Quilted Memories

Linda Hudson Hoagland

Quilted Memories

DEDICATION

Michael E. Hudson

Matthew A. Hudson

Quilted Memories

ACKNOWLEDGEMENTS

*Publish America (America Star) of Baltimore for originally publishing this book in 2011

*Victoria Fletcher, fellow author, for editing and formatting this book. She also developed the cover design for the book.

*"Child Abuse: The Other Victim" - Published in Internationally Yours: Prize-Winning Stories, 2006

*"He Touched Me"- Published in Bluestone Review, 2005

*"Nighttime at the Outhouse" - Published in Miners' Lamps and Cold Mountain Winters, 2008

*"Old Man Hudson Wants His Land Back" - Published in Cold Outhouses and Kerosene Lamps, 2009

*"Our Christmas House" - Published in Front Porch, 2004

*"Quilt Pieces" - Published in Wordsmith 2010

*"Secret Santa" - Published as "Next Year Will Be Better" in Christmas Blooms, 2008

*"Size 12" - Published in Still Moments, 2004

*"The Ladder" - Internet at www.storyhouse.org

*"The Mailbox - Published in CMR (Clinch Mountain Review) 2004

*"The Night Walk" - 2nd Place in Wild Violet First Annual Fiction Contest 2004

Internet at www.wildviolet.net

*"Visiting Karin" - Published in CMR, 2007

Quilted Memories

CHAPTER 1

THE CAROUSEL

"Ellen, you're not doing that right. Give it to me and get out of here," were the not so endearing words I often heard from my mother. These long unheard and hopefully forgotten words surfaced when I looked at the quilt.

It had belonged to my mother, the quilt, I mean. When she died, I got everything because I had taken care of her for all those many years without any help or support from my brother who lived in another state. It was only right, you know.

She wasn't easy to take care of because she was cantankerous and fractious always wanting to argue with me. I didn't want to argue. I would leave the room when she would start up. I just didn't want to hear her mouth run all the time.

She never had anything good to say. I always did something; I mean, everything wrong, no matter what it was. I learned to live with it. I didn't have to like it but I had to live with it.

When I was a teenager, many years earlier, I can remember my girlfriend telling me that she wished she had a mother like mine. She told me how lucky I was because my mother was always around to take care of my brother and me. I don't guess I knew how lucky I was then, but it sure would have been nice to have had that same nice mother instead of the cranky old hag of a woman that died.

I gazed at the quilt and permitted my thoughts to escape into another world filled with yesterday.

I could see the horses as plain as day. They were yellow; bright, bold yellow sporting a vivid crimson bridle. They were holding their mouths open as they held the bits between their teeth. They appeared to be running, sucking in wind through their mouths, flaring their large, round nostrils, with their ears back and their manes flying. They didn't look like happy horses enjoying the exercise. They looked frightened with dark, round eyes wide open to see what was lurking ahead- waiting.

The horses would spin and spin circling slowly at first but gradually building up speed until there was no way I could hang on to the pole. If I let go, I would fly off into the black hole of space sinking forever into the depths of nothingness.

The music that emanated from the circling horses was not the happy-go-lucky sound I would expect at a carnival or county fair. It was a speeded up version of a funeral dirge. That horrible sound made me want to cry and hide from the heavy burden of the so-called music.

I could see nothing else as if that were the only operating mechanical object in my world. I turned my head back and forth looking, searching for something else, anything else that would let me know that I and this ring of horses, this weird carousel, were not the only things functioning in my world.

The spinning continued and the speed increased.

I flung my head back and forth, back and forth, with the speed of the flings increasing to match the spinning of the horses.

I could no longer control the movement of my head. My hands and feet started moving, kicking out to try to stop the spinning of the horses and the momentum of the movements of my body.

"Stop, please stop!" I screamed into the night.

The carousel was gone.

I sat up at a ninety degree angle on my bed drenched in the sweat of fear, not the sweet smelling sissy perspiration that I had been told to call it since childhood.

I blinked my eyes slowly to make sure I was awake. I pinched my arm hoping to feel the pain.

Quilted Memories

When I opened my eyes again I was staring into total darkness.

Had I fallen off the carousel? Had the speed of the spinning horses thrown me into space to float around until I died or was killed by whomever or whatever found me in the total blackness?

Before I dove into total and complete panic, I took a slow, deep breath and focused my vision so that I might accept the images that my eyes were actually seeing.

There was light, somewhere there was light. I could see it.

I was awake and sitting on my bed.

I was not floating in the black hole of space to my death.

At least, not yet.

I reached out my hand to find my bedside lamp.

With a click, my bedroom exploded with light.

I glanced at the alarm clock that was ticking loudly beside the lamp and saw the time to be two o'clock in the wee hours of morning.

I climbed off of my bed, pulled a blanket from the closet, grabbed my pillow, and marched my tired but wide-awake body to the living room where I would watch television until I was overtaken, once more, by the need to sleep.

While I heard the mindless droning of the television and watched the constant changing of light intensity caused by the scenes being displayed on the screen, my mind sifted through the events of the previous day that had ended trying to find out why I was dreaming of the monster carousel.

"Ellen, make some breakfast, now," screamed a harsh, raspy voice from down the narrow hallway that led to the rear of the mobile home, or trailer as I referred to it.

"What do you want to eat?"

"You know what I want."

"Okay, okay," I growled in response.

I reached under the kitchen range and retrieved a fry pan for the preparation of two eggs fried in lard. I would also have to lightly toast two slices of bread and slather them excessively with butter then coat them thickly with strawberry preserves. This is what my mother ate for breakfast on a regular basis. No amount of talk could persuade her to change her menu.

"Mom, come get your breakfast," I shouted down the narrow hallway.

"Bring it to me," demanded the disembodied voice.

"You've got to walk, Mom. If you don't use your legs, you will lose the ability to get around. You know that. Now, come to the table," I pleaded knowing I would have to carry the food down the hall to my mother's room.

It was a constant battle getting my mother to move

her massive body around a bit so that she would be able to continue to navigate on her own.

I placed the food on a tray and carried it to mother's room where I deposited it onto the small wooden table that was designed and built for that purpose.

"Mom, you need to start eating cereal or fruit for breakfast. You know the lard and butter are bad for you."

"I'll eat what I like."

"You won't if I don't fix it for you, will you?"

"I'll make it myself. Don't threaten me, Ellen. Get out of here and leave me alone."

"I'll be glad to do that as soon as your baby-sitter gets here," I said as I turned on my heel and left the room.

"None of that should have caused the weird carousel to appear," I thought as the memories continued to play in my head.

The mother sitter did not show up and I was forced to stay home from work. It's not that I didn't want to stay home and care for my mother, but I couldn't afford to miss another day without taking a chance that I might be fired.

"Mom, I don't think your health care worker is coming by today. Did she say anything to you about not being here?"

"Yeah, she said she had to be in court for something. I can't remember what it was."

"Why didn't you tell me so I could find someone else to stay with you?" I asked angrily.

"You're supposed to know everything. I didn't think I had to tell you. Now, get out of here."

"Aw, Mom, why do you do this to me?" I pleaded.

"Because you're a thief. You've stolen all of my money. You keep me locked up in this house and won't let me go anywhere. I hate you, Ellen," screamed my mother as I stood at the doorway feeling the angry, hurtful tears streaming down my reddened cheeks.

I turned and left the room mumbling to myself as I tried to smooth over the ugly words my mother had spewed at me.

"The doctor told me that people with brain injuries, and that's exactly what Alzheimer's is, blame those they love the most with everything bad that is happening. They accuse their loved one of stealing and spying and hurting them," I recited from memory. "Why do I let her continue to hurt me?"

"I'm human, that's why," I replied automatically without giving the topic further thought.

I called into work and explained I would be late because I had to locate a mother sitter. They weren't happy about it, but neither was I.

When I went back later in the morning to check on my mother, I discovered she was missing from her room. My mother had propelled herself along the narrow hallway to the bathroom.

While mother was out of the room, I decided to change the sheets and generally straighten up a bit.

As I turned to leave the room my hand hit the glass music box that I had given mother many years earlier. It crashed to the floor and broke into many tiny pieces that would be impossible to reassemble.

Quickly I ran to retrieve the broom and dustpan. I wanted to remove the breakage before mother could comment about it.

"Ellen, what were you doing in my room?" screamed my mother down the narrow hallway.

"Making the bed, Mom. That's all."

"What did you break? I heard something break. What was it?"

"Nothing, Mom. I knocked a book off the table," I lied to prevent an ugly argument.

"Make me some lunch."

"It's not time for lunch yet."

"I want some soup, some cream of chicken soup, Ellen. I want it now."

"Okay, Mom, okay. I'll ask Donna to make it for you when she gets here."

Donna was the afternoon mother sitter. I wasn't able to pay to have one person sit all day so I had to have it done in shifts allowing the Commission on Aging to foot part of the bill.

When I arrived at work, the frowns were evident because I was late, but there was nothing I could do about that except live with it.

I tried my best to cram a whole day's worth of work into four hours. That's how it had to be.

When my work day ended I went back home to my mother and my second full time job of taking care of family and home not to mention the bills and whatever crisis occurred each day.

I couldn't imagine why I was dreaming of an evil carousel. My mind brought up no thoughts of horses, or carnivals, or fairs, or merry-go-rounds, or fun of any kind. I shouldn't be dreaming about a carousel at all.

After a fitful night, I went to work on time.

My mind kept wandering back to the nightmare, the dream, of the speeding carousel.

The horses didn't look like content, working horses. They were evil, sneering animals that were extremely unhappy.

The music was not the kind associated with the lighthearted, lively tunes that roared from the fun, family carousel. The music from my dream, my nightmare was a dirge, more like a background tune played at a funeral. It would crescendo into loud overbearing noise that would threaten to deafen the bystander. Not good music, it played evil, fear producing sounds that penetrated my soul.

15

"Ellen, is there something wrong?" asked Sandy, my office coworker.

"No, I was just thinking about the dream I had last night. It was a dilly."

"What kind of dream was it?"

"More like a nightmare. I really can't figure out why I dreamed such a strange dream. It was about horses on a carousel that was running out of control."

"You must have seen a horse or something that reminded you of a carousel that same day before you went to bed."

"That's what I thought, but I could think of nothing that was even remotely related."

"It's going to be something unrelated then, just an idea, like maybe a spinning top that reminded you of the spinning of the carousel."

"Yeah, maybe," I responded when my mind tried to focus in on a fleeting thought but it was gone from my memory before I actually had a chance to retrieve it.

"I hope you get some sleep tonight. You really look tired, Ellen."

"I hope so, too. I am tired, really tired. Seems like I have too much on my mind what with my mother and all the worries related to her care and well-being. Ignoring the fact that she tells me she hates me daily, it is really hard to take care of a person who doesn't want your help."

"That's got to be rough."

"It is."

The workday seemed to drag on forever because I was tired and needed sleep.

"Ellen, I'm hungry. Fix me something to eat."

"Okay, Mom, just let me get inside the door before you start telling me to do something,"

I said as I ran to my bedroom to change from my work clothes.

"I want something good to eat. Not any of the good-for-you stuff you've been trying to kill me with."

"What do you want?"

"I want to clean that turkey carcass you cooked this past weekend. I want to pick the bones clean."

"Mom, I'm going to throw that out after I remove all of the leftover meat. I'll make you a turkey sandwich."

"No, I don't want a sandwich. I want you to heat the carcass after you cut off what you want and let me pick at what I want. Now, that's what I want, Ellen. I mean it."

I did what my mother wanted. I placed the heated turkey carcass on a platter and then, after making mother walk to the kitchen table, I set the whole warm carcass in front of mother so she could make her mess.

That's exactly what she did. She had drippings splattered all over the table and onto the floor, but my mother was happy. She got what she wanted.

I wanted to tell my mother about the broken music box but I decided to wait another day. I wasn't up to the ugly words that I would hear.

After cleaning up the mess mother made and washing some of the never disappearing pile of clothes, I climbed into bed at midnight. Five o'clock would come too early. I knew I had to get to bed earlier but I hadn't been able to discover how I could.

It was back.

The carousel was taunting me, diving at me, as I stood to the side and watched it spin and whirl faster and faster. I knew carousels couldn't move. They couldn't glide around in the air and punch and jab at me like a frenzied boxer. I knew it couldn't be happening- but it was.

The yellow horses were glowing with the brightness of burning, searing, blinding light. The teeth of the fierce animals were obtusely large as they loudly gnashed at the bits clamped between the upper and lower rows of teeth. The speed of the spinning carousel was causing the horses to froth and snort as they searched for air.

Suddenly the carousel shattered.

The whole picture tinkled to the ground like the glass from a broken window pane.

I knew what was causing the dream - the nightmare. My life was spinning out of control and I knew I had to start setting things straight.

"Mom, I broke your music box, the one with the horses, a couple of days ago. I didn't mean to do it. My arm brushed against it when I left your room after making your bed."

"I know, Ellen. I was wondering when you were going to tell me."

"You aren't mad at me, are you?"

"No, I know you didn't mean to do it."

"I've got to go to work now. Mary, your morning care giver will be here soon."

I walked out of my mother's bedroom and marveled at the contrasts that Alzheimer's patients and their families faced each day.

Today, my mother didn't hate me. Perhaps my mother might even love me.

I didn't want to think about what tomorrow might bring.

****

She started her day early, too early, because the moment she climbed out of bed she began her vigil of watching. She knew it was too early to watch but she couldn't stop herself. She would watch and wait, watch and wait, until the light disappeared from the sky.

Mom's reason for existence was to keep a constant vigil over her mailbox. It wasn't a special mailbox. It wasn't magical in any way. It was just a mailbox.

At the first light of dawn, mom would drag herself up from the depths of dream filled sleep. She couldn't always remember the dreams. The dreams were so active and explosive with sights and sounds from which she would wake up exhausted as if she had worked all night.

Mom's eyes would spring open suddenly. She would be wide-eyed, looking around as if she were trying to find the reason she was awake. She strained her ears listening for a sound that had caused her to awaken. It must have come from inside her dreams. That was the only reason she could think of for the sudden awakening.

Even if mom were tired and sleepy she wouldn't or couldn't go back to sleep because she had to watch and wait. She had to be where she could see the mailbox. She had to wait for her letter.

Mom would force her feet to move from under the comfort of the covers until they touched the cold, vinyl-clad floor. She would sit on the edge of the bed until her brain adjusted to waking up. She would pull her bulky body from the bed rising slowly until she was standing straight.

Mom placed her hand against both the walls seeking support in the narrow hallway as she lumbered her way to the bathroom that was located next to her small bedroom in the old trailer. Her old trailer bought and paid for with her own money.

After relieving her bladder of an overload of fluid and splashing cold water onto her face, mom would pull her homemade housedress over her head, run a large, multi-tooth comb through her mostly gray hair, and walk into the living room. There she would plant her three hundred pound bulk into her lift chair directly in front of the door that led from the living room to the front porch. She kept her front door open winter and summer so she could see her mailbox any time she glanced in that direction.

That's where my mom would wait and watch.

Precisely at eight o'clock each morning, mom would rise from her lift chair and prepare her breakfast. She was still able to get around but she knew that, too, was rapidly coming to an end. It hadn't happened yet. She could still take care of herself. She and Peanut were just fine.

When she was in the kitchen, with the help of P-diddy, an affectionate nickname for Peanut, her Chihuahua mix dog, she could still keep an eye open for any activity in the front of her house. The slightest movement by anyone or anything would start the dog into fits of loud, vicious sounding barking.

Mom knew she could count on P-diddy to help her, to let her know about any movement in front of her house. She knew of no one else that she could definitely count on for help, only P-diddy.

Mom's breakfast was almost always two eggs fried in lard with lots and lots of butter and jelly or jam on her toast.

Mom knew it was bad for her but she was already old, so she was filling her life with the things she liked. It didn't matter to her that the eggs were filled with cholesterol, as was the lard. It didn't matter to her that she should have substituted special margarine for the real butter she loved to eat. What mattered to her was that she liked what she ate.

Of course, none of the death inducing food products was working, so mom had to sit and wait and watch. What else could she do? She was so old, so alone.

Whatever mom ate was shared with P-diddy. The dog had taken on the round appearance of his master, but that didn't matter because P-diddy was old, too.

After breakfast, mom would leave the plate and fork sitting on the table next to her chair. She would put them into the kitchen sink to wash later when she had to get up again to go to the bathroom.

Mom reached for the remote control to change the channel on her television, which along with reading romance novels, was her only form of entertainment.

"P-diddy, it's time for *Little House on the Prairie*," she told her dog every morning at nine o'clock.

Mom had seen the episode that was airing on Channel 8 at least six times, but that didn't matter. She liked *Little House* and she would watch the same episode over and over again never searching the other channels for something different. She watched the television show as it began daily with the enthusiasm one would display for the excitement of seeing a much-anticipated new episode of a favorite television series. Each episode was watched again and again with that very same enthusiasm.

After *Little House* mom would switch off the television, pick up her paperback romance novel, and lose herself in the make-believe lives of others.

Mom's life had never, ever been like the stories she read in her romance novels. It was too late to think that wonderful feelings of being swept off your feet in love would ever happen to her. She knew she could always enjoy reading about the happiness of others. She could always dream of what her life would have been like if the same joyful events that happened in her reading might have happened to her. It was too late to live those dreams. Never the less, she enjoyed her thoughts and wishes. That's all she had, she thought; just thoughts and wishes and her romance novels full of make believe lives.

Before long mom was nodding off to sleep. Her head had dropped forward with her chin resting as close to her chest as her double chin would allow. Her neck was short so there wasn't enough strain to cause the pain that would awaken her.

Mom's light snore could be heard in every room of her home but who would care? Not the lonely mom, who had only P-diddy to love her, no one else loved her except maybe her daughter.

Mom's bifocals had been knocked slightly off kilter and her right hand continued to hold the paperback novel but her grasp was loosening and the book was sliding ever so slowly toward the floor.

When the book finally hit the floor, mom heard the noise and roused herself from her nap.

"P-diddy, you let me go to sleep," she admonished her faithful pet.

The dog jumped from his position on the sofa to his master's lap where he awaited the loving attention he expected to receive every time mom uttered his name in the soft loving tone.

"My P-diddy, my baby, my little P-diddy," whispered mom as she hugged her pet to her chest.

Mom reached for the television remote. She pressed the button for the power and the screen came alive with *The Price Is Right.*

Mom glanced at *The Price Is Right* as she thought about what she would have for lunch.

It wasn't going to be anything elaborate. Mom didn't do those kinds of lunches anymore. She used to make a big lunch every day when dad was alive, but no more. He had been dead for several years and now she was waiting her turn.

"Let's have a bowl of cream of chicken soup, P-diddy. I'll get you some bologna so you don't have to eat the soup."

At twelve o'clock after *The Price Is Right* had gone off the air to be replaced by the local news, mom shuffled to the kitchen.

Mom pulled her favorite soup pan from under the sink and opened the can of condensed soup. Cream of chicken soup was her favorite. She ate it every day.

She heated the pan filled with the contents of the can and the required water. Mom slowly stirred the soup. She poked her finger into the liquid every few seconds to test the hotness of the soup. She only wanted the soup to get warm. She didn't want it to boil. It was much too hot to eat if it reached the boiling point.

Mom poured her soup into a bowl into which she dropped a handful of small soup crackers to absorb some of the liquid.

Mom opened the refrigerator to get herself a can of 7-UP. She shoved the 7-UP into her dress pocket along with the soupspoon. She needed a free hand to carry P-diddy's two slices of bologna.

"Come on, boy. Let's eat."

Mom shuffled back to her chair where she sat holding her soup in one hand and the spoon in the other. When she tired of holding the soup bowl, she would let it rest atop her protruding stomach that served as a makeshift table.

The dog had not barked all morning. There had been no activity near her mailbox. The delivery had not arrived yet so mom would continue to watch and wait.

It was going to come. Her letter would get there soon. Mom certainly had waited a long time but another day was all right, for now anyway.

Mom sat in her chair and watched out the clear window of the storm door. She was comfortable but there had been many days, especially in the dead of winter, when she had to wrap a blanket around her body to stay warm.

The wind would whistle around the edges of the door blowing the winter's chill inside her home directly at her.

Mom wouldn't close the door during daylight hours because she wouldn't be able to see the mailbox. She had to see the mailbox. She had to watch and wait for the delivery of the letter.

Again mom started dozing in her lift chair. It was hard to keep a constant watch without succumbing to the fatigue that would overtake her.

P-diddy sprang from his resting-place on the sofa and viciously barked at movement in front of the house.

Mom opened her eyes and saw the mail carrier drive passed the mailbox. He didn't stop to deliver the letter for which mom was waiting.

"Sh-sh-sh, P-diddy. He's gone. He didn't even stop. Be quiet, boy. Maybe it will be delivered later today by a different mail carrier. We'll wait and see, P-diddy."

Mom glanced at the television and saw that her favorite show was beginning.

"P-diddy, *Murder She Wrote* is on. Let's watch it."

The dog jumped back onto the sofa and curled up to sleep in his favorite resting-place.

The day was fading to evening and mom no longer felt the need to watch the mailbox. She knew there would be no more mail deliveries that day. She would continue her watching and waiting tomorrow. It would be delivered then. She was sure of it.

"Mom, why do you watch that mailbox all day long?"

She looked me at as if I were a stranger asking her the question.

"I have to."

"Why?"

"I'm expecting to get a letter from my daughter any day now."

"I'm your daughter, mom."

"No-o-o-o, you're not a nice person. You're a thief. You stole all my money. You made me sell my house. You're not my daughter. Ellen will be writing me a letter soon asking me to live with her."

"I'm Ellen and you are living with me."

"She will write to me soon and ask me and P-diddy to come and stay with her."

"You are, mom. You are living with Ellen. I am Ellen. P-diddy is living here, too. Why can't you understand that? Why can't you understand that the mailbox you stare at every hour of every day doesn't belong to this family? We get our mail at the post office. Why can't you understand that, mom? We are living in my house, not your ratty old trailer. Why can't you understand that?"

"I don't want you to stay with me any longer. I'm going to go live with my daughter and her family. Get out of here."

"I can't, mom. This is my home. You are living with me. I'm your daughter," I said as I fought the tears that were flowing down my cheeks.

"Ellen will write soon."

"How can I get through to you?"

I knew the answer to that question was one that would not be answered in my mother's lifetime. Old age was destroying my mother's mind, cutting off parts of her brain forever. It was so hard to watch my mother fade away as each day passed.

I knew I would have to institutionalize my mother soon, but until then, I wanted to share as many days as I possibly could with her.

I would let my mother sit in her lift chair and wait for a letter to be delivered to the mailbox that wasn't hers from the daughter who was already here.

Mom remembered the daughter that she knew in the past, not the daughter of the present.

****

We fought day after day over the fact that she wouldn't bathe. She kept telling me she wasn't able to, but I knew better. She could stand next to the kitchen range heating up her cream of chicken soup every day. I knew she could stand in the shower to get clean. She didn't want to be clean. She wanted to keep forever the strong odor that permeated her room caused by the wrinkles of skin that would sweat from heat and the urine that leaked all over her bedclothes despite any precautions I tried to take to prevent the odors from building up.

Plainly, she smelled bad and the stench permeated the entire house. I would go to work with the smell of my mother on my clothes and I couldn't get rid of it. No amount of deodorant or disinfectant spray would get rid of the stink.

"Mom, please, you've got to take a bath. You stink so bad," I cried as I tried to get her to cooperate.

"I don't smell anything."

"Of course you don't. You've wallowed in the mess and stink for so long that it smells natural to you," I said angrily.

"You just want to search my room and steal my money."

"You don't have any money. How can I steal it?"

Finally, I had to beg the doctor to make a telephone call and obtain the services of a home health organization and have it billed to Medicare. I wanted a woman sent to the house every day to help my mother take a shower because she wouldn't let me do it. That same home health worker would change her bedclothes every day and clean her room at bit. The smell finally became confined to her room only. I wasn't embarrassed to ask a friend to the house for a visit.

There was still an old person smell in the house but it was nothing like the nasty, filthy, stinky smell that was there before the home health lady started making regular visits.

I wanted so very much to remember the good times I had with my mother but the bad times of her final years were overriding any good memories.

CHAPTER 2

THE DRESS PATTERN

I looked at the quilt that had been stored in the closet out of sight for so long that I had forgotten she ever owned it.

My sister-in-law made the quilt. It was patterned with many colorful blocks about four inches square that were tacked to the quilt backing with colorful pieces of yarn. My mother had given my sister-in-law most of the fabric that was used in making the colorful blocks.

The colorful pieces of cloth represented a four inch square of my history, my mother's history, my family's history, each pieced together into a beautiful handmade quilt. The workmanship was good. It was all pieced by a hand held needle. None of the quilt ever touched a sewing machine. Each individual block was sewn into place twice so that it would never come apart.

I would say that there was love sewn throughout the quilt under normal circumstances, but in this case, I can't.

My sister-in-law did not love my mother. They hardly knew each other. After all, she was my brother's third wife.

I unfolded the quilt and placed my hand on a couple of the blocks of color. It almost felt alive, breathing in the warmth of my touch.

"I think I'll put this on my bed right now," I mumbled as I jerked at my bedclothes.

When I crawled into bed, I was past exhaustion. It seemed that I had spent the entire work day putting out fires; not physically, but mentally I was facing one major disaster after another at the office. Items didn't get ordered when they were supposed to. Items were coming in without orders from me meaning they were ordered by others without the necessary paperwork. I was late getting a report to the boss that I had been told about that morning. Talk about the last minute. If anything could go wrong, it did.

The quilt was a warm welcoming reminder that some things didn't change. It reminded me that my whole life was not a disaster, only that day at work was a little on the rough side.

Suddenly I was asleep. My mind had finally located the stop, or perhaps it was the pause, button and allowed sleep to overtake the instant replays of all of my mistakes.

I snuggled down under the quilt waiting for good dreams to fill my head during the remainder of the night.

My mind focused on a colorful square that had been

sewn into the quilt.

The block of fabric in focus was left over from the dress my mother had made for herself. She always made her dresses and they all looked the same. The only difference I ever saw was the color of the fabric.

The block was deep dark red with tiny little blue designs throughout the field of deep dark red. I believe the designs were flowers but they were so small that they looked almost like blue misshaped dots. The deep dark red block rippled and waved as if it were a flag being buffeted by the wind. It floated along, rippling and waving. It started floating forward, then back, then forward again, until it steadied itself to form a background. It looked like a room wallpapered with the deep dark red and blue spotted designs.

"When do you plan to clean up this mess?" shouted my angry father as he looked at my mother.

"What's the matter, Walter? I cleaned that up. The kids must have made this mess after I was finished in here and was doing something else," she sputtered.

I heard the conversation that was taking place. If you were in the house, you wouldn't have been able to avoid the cross words being exchanged.

"We didn't do anything, Dad," I butted into the argument as I tried to defend myself and my brother.

"Tommie, get this cleaned up right now!" my dad shouted at my mother. Tommie was a pet name for my mother based on her maiden name of Thompson.

"I'll do it, Dad," I said as I started pulling the paper trash from the window seat. I wadded up the newspapers and brown paper bags and threw them into the trash can.

It seemed like I was always cleaning up after mom. Somehow this picture was all wrong. I really believed I shouldn't be cleaning up after her, not when she was a strong, healthy woman in her late thirties. It had always been that way. I couldn't remember when I wasn't embarrassed by the way the house looked.

Dad walked out of the house towards the out building where he stored his garden tools. He grabbed a hoe and starting working in the potato patch. He chopped the weeds at a rapid pace until he had worked out all of his frustration. Then he slowed down to a more normal pace and continued hoeing in the garden until long after sunset.

"Ellen, where did you put my dress pattern?" mom asked me the next morning.

"What dress pattern?"

"The one I had lying on the window seat."

"All I saw were newspapers," I said defensively.

"My pattern was cut out of newspapers. What did you do with it?"

"I threw all of the newspapers in the garbage. You watched me do it. Why didn't you tell me it was your dress pattern?"

"You shouldn't be touching things that don't belong to you," she said sternly.

"Dad wanted the place cleaned up. You told him we made the mess. You know that we didn't. You did it. Why didn't you tell him the truth?"

"I did tell him the truth. I cleaned it up earlier."

"How much earlier? You didn't do it that morning."

"I didn't tell him I did it that morning."

"Mom, if I didn't clean up after you, dad would have left long ago. I'm sorry about your old pattern. You need to put your things where they belong when you're finished working with them."

"I did. They belong exactly where I had them."

"On the window seat?"

"If that's where I want to keep my pattern, then that's where it belongs."

I stalked out of the room knowing that I had lost the battle again.

The deep dark red fabric with the blue misshaped dots floated away from the wall pushing forward, forward, closer to my eyes. I was getting nauseous from watching the motion of the fabric. When I could almost feel the fabric fluttering in my face I jerked myself awake.

I shook my head from side to side trying my level best to clear away the cobwebs that I thought were caused by the fitful sleep filled with nightmares.

"Why on earth had I dreamed about my mother and

the dress pattern that I had tossed into the trash?" I asked my mirrored reflection when I stood in front of the bathroom basin. "Must have been the quilt. I must have been thinking about her when I went to sleep."

That sounded like a logical answer, I thought as I crawled back under the covers of my bed.

A couple of nights of peaceful sleep were enjoyed before I dreamed again about the past.

The walls of this dream were sheer and gauzy. They had the color of the blue skies and were decorated with puffy white clouds with scalloped, lacey edges.

"Mommy, can I join the Brownies?" I asked with my head hung down because I knew, deep down in my heart I knew, what the answer would be.

"You have to ask your daddy," she said with a smile.

"Will you ask him for me?" I begged.

"No, you need to ask him yourself," she answered smugly.

"I don't want to," I whined.

"Then you already know you can't join the Brownies."

I ran from the room hiding the tears that were rolling down my cheeks. I didn't want mommy to see me cry. I wasn't one of those girls who cried all the time to get what she wanted. Daddy had taught my brother and me that crying wasn't going to get us what we wanted. And believe me, crying didn't get us anywhere, not with daddy.

Daddy was working in the garden out behind the house. You had to cross the wooden bridge that daddy had built over the creek to get to the garden. I didn't like that bridge very much. It was well built and strong. It certainly wasn't going to fall into the creek if you walked across it. I didn't like the bridge anyway.

There were holes in the bed of the bridge. When daddy put the bridge together, he built spaces of about one to two inches between each board and I could look down between the boards and see the creek which had to be ten or fifteen feet further down to the bottom. If I had to walk across the bridge, I would step on each board carefully so that I wouldn't fall between the cracks which I knew was impossible but I was still scared.

I would have to wait until daddy put down his hoe when he was hot and sweaty and, above all, tired. That was not a good time to ask him anything, but I had no choice. I didn't ask at supper time because my brother was sitting at the table. I didn't want my brother to throw in his two cents about anything I wanted to do and I knew he would. He would remind mommy and daddy that they didn't let him join the Boy Scouts so it wouldn't be fair to let me join the Brownie Troop which was part of the Girl Scouts.

I waited forever. It was finally dark enough for daddy to come into the house to get cleaned up and ready for bed so he could get some sleep before he had to go to work the next morning. He left for work so early that he was long gone before my brother and I were pulled from bed to get ready for school.

"Daddy?" I said softly when he had finally settled himself down into his easy chair.

"What, Ellen?" he snapped at me.

"Nothing, Daddy. I just wanted to tell you that I love you," I said as I fought back the wave of tears that were pressing on my eyeballs from the backside.

"Ellen, don't bother your daddy now. Go on to bed," said my mother as she pushed me away from daddy.

"I can't go to bed. Lee's sitting on it."

"Well, go sit in that chair and leave your daddy alone."

Telling me to go to bed didn't work very often because I had to sleep in the living room on a sofa bed with mommy and it was too early to chase everybody out of the living room so I could sleep. Daddy had a room of his own and so did my brother. It didn't seem fair to me that mommy and I had to sleep on the sofa bed but there was nothing I could do about the problem, not yet anyway.

Mommy didn't want me to get daddy all stirred up before he went to bed. He wasn't able to sleep very well most of the time. He always said it was because he was over tired. What actually caused his problem was that directly after supper each evening before he gathered himself to go outside and work in the garden, he would fall asleep in his easy chair snoring so loud that the rafters would rattle. If he got mad or upset with my brother or me or mommy before he went to bed, he slept even less. That's why she pushed me away from daddy and didn't want me to ask about the Brownies, but I had to have an answer before I went to school the next morning.

I didn't ask daddy before I went to sleep because of the mean looks mommy kept giving me.

"Walter, it's time to get up," whispered mommy as she called my daddy to get him up so he could get ready for work.

I was awake most of the night trying to make sure I was up and awake when daddy was getting ready for work. I was perfectly still making no movements when my mommy was in the room because I didn't want her to know I wasn't asleep.

I heard the bedroom door open and watched daddy as he weaved his way through the living room around my bed where I wasn't sleeping on his way to the bathroom. I knew better than to ask him then, bathroom duties came first.

I was starting to doze off so I jerked myself awake. I didn't want mommy to know I was awake so I knew I couldn't move around very much.

I heard him leave the bathroom and walk to the dining room table where he would wait for mommy to place his breakfast consisting of two fried eggs over easy, two pieces of bacon, and toast in front of him. His ever present cup of black coffee was already on the table.

Mommy was in the kitchen. Now was the time.

"Daddy," I said softly without any kind of a whine, "can I join the Brownies?"

"What's a Brownie?" he asked as he took of sip of his coffee that had been poured into the saucer for cooling and then back into the cup for drinking.

"It's the beginning part of Girl Scouts," I explained as I stood in front of my father in my nightgown with my fingers crossed tightly.

"No, Ellen, you can't. It costs too much."

I knew he would say no. That's why I wanted mommy to ask for me. She knew he would say no. That's why she didn't ask.

I didn't beg or plead. It would do no good. Lee hadn't been able to join the Boy Scouts so I knew the same fate was in store for me.

I whirled around and crawled back into bed where I tried to will myself to sleep but sleep wouldn't come. The torrent of silent wet tears kept me from going to sleep.

I went to school and watched all of the other little girls in my class talk and whisper about joining the Brownie Troop. I acted like I didn't care, but they all knew it was a lie. I did care. I really cared a big bunch and I would remember this for the rest of my life.

When I ran into the house after departing the big yellow school bus that stopped in front of the gate, mommy met me at the door and handed me my ballerina doll all decked out in a pretty new dress. The skirt of the dress was made out of the blue gauzy material that was sheer enough to see through. The bodice was made from white eyelet with scalloped edges. I suppose it was pretty

41

but I didn't want a new doll dress, I wanted to join the Brownies with my friends. I wanted to be like them. I didn't want to be different. I was tired of being different. We couldn't afford any extras in our lives, so that made us different. We were poor and we admitted to being poor.

I threw the doll onto the sofa and ran down to the basement. It was the only place I could think of where I could be alone.

I cried and cried until I felt like I was choking on my tears. I tried to catch my breath but I couldn't. Something or someone was pushing against my throat not letting me breathe. I struggled and fought pushing at the object that was trying to stop me from breathing.

I screamed.

I woke up with the quilt bunched up across my neck and I had somehow gotten the quilt wrapped around me in such a manner that it tightened its pressure on my neck with any and every movement I made.

I jerked myself up from the bed allowing the ends to loosen and fall away from behind my back. I shoved the quilt away from me, as far away from me as I could push it without actually letting it fall to the floor.

I forced myself to breathe slowly, calming me before I climbed out of bed to go to the bathroom.

"Why was I dreaming about the doll dress?" I asked the walls that surrounded me.

The struggle for breath, the fear of dying reminded me

of why I'm afraid of water.

The voice was grating on my nerves. It was telling me to do something I wasn't sure I could do.

"Aren't you getting in the water?"

"Yeah, give me a minute..."

I remembered the last time...

I watched the other kids having a great time in water that was too deep for me. I started to bounce toward them in my own dangerous water ballet.

My head went under the water.

I couldn't get my head up from under the sparkling liquid.

A hand...there was a hand on my head.

Air – I needed air.

I thrashed around until I bounced to the top...

"Come on, Ellen, don't be a chicken."

"Okay, okay!" I shouted as I started running toward the edge of the pool.

I wasn't going to jump into the water. I just wanted them to think that I was. I wasn't going to give anybody a second chance at trying to drown me.

As soon as I reached the edge just prior to entering the pool with a flying leap, I forced my legs to stop functioning and came to a dead stop.

"I can't get in right now. I have a stomach ache," I shouted as I clutched at my belly while I doubled over in pain, pain that wasn't there, not in my stomach anyway.

"Chicken, chicken, chicken!!!" came the shouts from the pool as my classmates and so-called friends chose to make fun of me.

Fear, dread, revulsion, panic, the need to vomit, all of those vile, repulsive feelings traversed my body as I fought back the memories of almost dying.

The stomach ache had become real, as I watched those kids that were leering at me and calling me names.

I collapsed to the concrete surface that served as an apron to the water, that same water that I feared so much.

"Hey, you! You, laying there on the edge of the pool! Are you okay?" shouted the lifeguard when he saw me fall to the concrete.

I couldn't answer. I was afraid my roiling innards were to spew forth the contents of my entire body.

Eventually Genevieve, another one of the outcasts to the super society of thoughtless females that attended my school, came to my side.

"Ellen, Ellen, are you sick?"

"I have a stomach ache," I whispered as I struggled to sit up.

"Hey, you, girl!" the lifeguard shouted again without putting forth the effort to climb off of his high tower. "Are you sick?"

I shook my head from side to side so he would stop hollering at me and embarrassing me to death.

"Let's get out of the sun," suggested Genevieve as she helped me up to lead me away from the pool.

My stomach was finally beginning to stop the roiling and I wasn't afraid to talk, not to Genevieve anyway,

"Are you afraid of the water?"

"No, I'm afraid of the people in the water."

"Why?"

"Someone tried to drown me the last time I was here. I really can't swim so I try to stay in the water that isn't above my head."

"How did you almost drown?"

"Well, I was following the crowd of girls and they were heading toward the deep water. They knew I couldn't swim because I told them so. They went to the deep water on purpose knowing that I would have to struggle to keep up," I said as tears started rolling down my cheeks.

"Okay, then what?"

"I went under the water and I felt a hand on my head holding me under. I really thought I was going to drown," I sobbed.

"But you didn't, did you? Did they know how scared you were? Did you say anything to anybody about being held down under the water?"

"No, I didn't say anything to anybody because when I reached the top and the air, no one was near me."

"Someone was just trying to scare you."

"Well, they did a good job."

"Let's get in the water now. I'll stay close to you. I promise you won't drown."

"I don't know..."

"We have to do it. They will never give you any peace if you don't get back into the water."

"I'll get back in the water. Someday. I know I will."

"You have to do it today, Ellen. Or, you'll never do it again."

"Who made you my boss? You can't tell me what I have to do," I said as I felt my temper building.

"I'm not your boss. I'm not telling you what to do except that if you don't get in that water today, you never will. If you come to the pool with me the next time I can get a ride here, I'll try to teach you to swim."

"Why are you being so nice?"

"I know what it feels like to be left out. I just moved here a couple of months ago and you are about the only who has spoken to me at school. This is a real hard place to get to know anybody."

"Yes, it is. Once you get to know them, you might even wish you hadn't."

"Are you going to do it? Get in the pool?"

"Give me a minute to think about it."

"Don't think too long."

"Okay, okay," I said with a smile.

Genevieve was really a nice person, I thought as I struggled to make up my mind about jumping in the water and facing those who tried to drown me. Maybe it was only one of them who held me under but I was sure the others were watching as I thrashed around searching for air.

"Are you ready?" Genevieve asked me as she pulled on my hand to get me up from my sitting position.

"I guess so. I'm as ready as I'm ever going to be."

We ran to the pool's edge and jumped in without hesitation. It was something I had to do and I knew that even without the reminder from Genevieve.

I felt the water surround me like a warm blanket but I wasn't comfortable. I could endure it for a while so I could enjoy Genevieve's company. I smiled and splashed around like it was the most fun I had ever had in my life but every time I floated into water that was more than chest high I panicked, not outwardly, no one near me knew the fear that was cruising through my blood infiltrating my entire body and soul.

"See, it's not so bad, is it?"

"No, not when you have a friend with you. It's really fun when you're with someone who cares."

Genevieve and I played in the water away from the snobbery sisters' sorority otherwise known as my classmates.

"Genevieve, they say at school that your mom and dad fight a lot and the cops are always at your house. It that true?"

"Yes, my mom and dad can't seem to get along with each other?"

"Why do they stay together?"

"Out of spite. They want to see how miserable they can make each other. That's why we haven't stayed in one place very long. Once the cops get called, we move."

"They don't hurt you, do they?"

"You mean hitting?"

I bobbed my head up and down as an answer.

"No, they don't hit me. My pain comes from all the ugly words they say to each other and to me."

"Like what?"

"I don't want to talk about it anymore, okay Ellen?"

"Sure, but I'm here for you anytime you need to talk."

"I've said enough already."

The remainder of the summer Genevieve and I were friends, close friends, and remained that way until Genevieve and her family moved away suddenly.

I never knew why they disappeared from our small town so quickly. I hoped it wasn't because someone had called the cops.

It was almost as if she had entered my life with only one purpose, and that was to be my friend when I desperately needed one.

Just as an added note, to this day I don't like to play in the water.

I made my bed and looked at the quilt that I had spread on the top. I was using the bright colorful quilt as a bedspread. It was so pretty and it held so many memories. It was a real shame that most of those memories were bad.

CHAPTER 3

CHILD ABUSE – REALLY?

I decided to launder the quilt to remove any scents or odors that might be encouraging my brain to dwell on bad thoughts. I knew a thorough normal washing in the machine wasn't going to do any harm to the colorful blocks because my sister-in-law had made sure her finished product was sturdy enough to withstand the abuse a washing machine would cause.

Once the quilt was dried and placed back on my bed, I noticed a slight bit of fading on some of the blocks but that could be expected. It smelled clean and fresh and beckoned me to crawl under and accept the warmth it had to offer.

After work I decided I needed a nap before tackling the remainder of the evening. The idea of a nap was unusual for me. Any sleep time during the day caused me sleeping problems at night so I tried to avoid placing myself in a horizontal position on the sofa or the bed.

It was the fresh clean quilt that enticed me to stretch out onto the bed and close my eyes for a few moments. Fifteen minutes, no longer, I wanted a fifteen minute power nap.

My eyes were closed before my head touched the pillow. The panorama of my past began to wind its way through my brain.

Dad was gone out of town to Indiana where he had found another job after getting laid off by the railroad. There were times I was glad when my dad was gone because he was so strict and set in his ways.

Were the whippings my brother and I received child abuse? I don't think so, but it did hurt.

A few years later, my brother discovered what a real accusation of child abuse meant.

"How can I prove that I didn't abuse my son?'

"Why didn't they check with me when my son made the accusation of child abuse?"

"Don't I have any rights?"

"What happens if my son is lying?"

"Will this stay on my record forever?"

These were questions my brother asked me when he was accused of abusing his sixteen-year-old son. I didn't know the answers to the questions so I did some research.

According to the information I received from the Virginia Department of Social Services, an accusation is made by either the child, a teacher, a friend, a neighbor, a doctor, or anybody who is interested enough to make a telephone call. A determination is made whether or not the report should be investigated. I understand this is a judgment call on the part of the recipient of the report. A child protective services worker is supposed to contact the parent or guardian and the child upon receiving a report of child abuse or neglect.

In my brother's case, the child who was his son made the report of child abuse; therefore most of the outside investigative work was bypassed. The case was automatically noted for investigation.

Without any warning, a social worker, set out to prove that my brother and his wife were child abusers by dropping in on them at their home. My brother was flabbergasted by the accusation that he was unduly harsh with the punishment that he meted out to his son. He felt he had done no more to his son, perhaps even less, that his own father had done to him; and he certainly did not feel that he himself was abused.

Yes – he used corporal punishment against his son when the misbehavior called for it.

Yes – he used other forms of punishment that included doing additional chores around the house that his son hated to do such as washing dishes and cleaning the kitchen floor.

Yes – he yelled at his son and perhaps called him "stupid" or "dumb" when his son made a ridiculous mistake.

No – there was no mental abuse issued by my brother against his son. The reverse would be the truth because his son was performing the abuse on his father and stepmother by pitting them against his other set of parents, his mother and stepfather, who were living in West Virginia.

My brother had no way of proving that he was not unduly harsh with the punishment he issued to his son. The only witnesses to the actions in question were my brother, his son, and my sister-in-law. As far as my brother knew, any marks left by the corporal punishment occurred when his son tried to run from him causing the blow to hit in an especially sensitive area or maybe they were self-inflicted.

The report was made and a file was established thereby placing a questionable blemish on my brother's record. He was then contacted by a social worker who went into his home with the attitude that he was already guilty and it was my brother's job to prove that he wasn't guilty.

The rights of my brother were in question from the moment the report was made. It appears that the state controls your right as a parent at the mere mention of child abuse, especially if that accusation comes from a child. My brother had the right to disprove this statement but he was fighting the law that leaned heavily on the side of his son.

My brother spoke with his son about being labeled a child abuser. After a long antagonistic conversation, my brother extracted from his son the reason for the accusation. His son wanted to go back to live with his mother who allowed him to do whatever he desired with only cursory supervision. My nephew said he used the child abuse route because when he moved in with his father, he had been told that this would be his last move back and forth between parents until he graduated from high school or moved out on his own. My nephew wanted the state to send him back to his mother so that neither parent would have a choice in the matter.

My brother asked his son to tell the social worker the truth but that did not happen. My brother told the social worker what his son had said and it was noted in the file. No further investigation was made because it was agreed by all concerned that my brother's son should go to live with his mother until he reached the age of eighteen.

As far as my brother's record of child abuse was concerned, a reason to suspect abuse was reported, but no clear and convincing evidence was discovered. The file was kept active for one year and then the information was destroyed.

Had convincing and clear evidence been uncovered of child abuse or neglect, the file would have remained active until ten years after his son's eighteenth birthday.

My brother feels that he was falsely accused and almost convicted with a lie that the Social Services Department willingly accepted.

The accusation caused a rift between father and son that will never be forgotten.

My brother questions the ease with which an accusation can be made and the "you're guilty" attitude that emanates from the employees of the Social Services Department.

The information that I gathered to help my brother with his dilemma proved to be of value to me when I was also accused of child abuse against my fourteen-year-old stepson.

My husband and I had been married for only two months when the accusation was made.

When my husband, Sonny, and I initially decided to be married, I happily acquired his three sons to go along with my two sons.

After a short time, his two younger sons decided they would prefer to live with their mother and arrangements were made to let them live where they wanted to be.

Ned, age fourteen, chose our home to be permanent, or so we thought.

Ned was a chronic bed wetter who had been checked by numerous doctors and psychologists for his problem. No reason, other than the fact that he was too lazy to get out of bed in the middle of the night, could be found to be the cause of the bedwetting.

This problem led to many harsh discussions and threats from both his father and me. We thought the problem was disappearing when I found no more wet underwear in the clothes hamper and no evidence of wetness on his mattress each morning when he left for school.

As it turns out, one afternoon when I was cleaning his room, I found the smelly, wet underwear hidden everywhere. I also discovered that every morning when Ned got out of bed, he would rotate his mattress so that the dry side would be on the top.

The strong smell of stale urine in the room was what had prompted me to clean it and try to locate the source of the odor.

When we confronted Ned, again, he grew very angry and started saying some very ugly, disrespectful remarks aimed at me because I wasn't his mother. I could see that Sonny was about to come out of his chair and deal with Ned physically, so I reached to the floor and grabbed a sponge rubber thong that I had been wearing and struck Ned with it on the side of his face. Ned backed down and apologized for his remarks and my husband settled himself in his chair. That was the only time this five-foot-two-inch stepmother ever struck the six-foot tall Ned while he lived in our home.

Soon after my confrontation with Ned, he too, wanted to go live with his mother. In order to go live with her, he had to have a good reason for leaving our home because his father and I had made it perfectly clear to him that when he chose to live with us, it would be permanent. If at any time he changed his mind and went to live with his mother, he would not be allowed to return to our house to live for any reason. I was not going to be used as a means of getting what he wanted any time he wanted it. I had seen that happen to too many children and parents. I didn't want to be a statistic.

When my husband went to visit his mother, Ned's grandmother, he was told that she didn't appreciate my abusing her grandson. He was also told that I had beaten him with a hard sole shoe.

Sonny explained to his mother what had actually happened and that there was no abuse what so ever involved. Sonny also told her that Ned was just angry with both of us because we were trying to stop his bedwetting.

Sonny's mother went to her grave believing that I abused her grandson because she refused to believe that Ned would lie to her.

As you can see from both incidents, the teenage boys used the system to their advantage. Whether or not there was actual abuse involved didn't matter because both boys got what they wanted and our fear, as parents, of being labeled a child abuser let them win.

When I awoke from my dream, I was lying face down on the quilt and my eyes were focused on the yellowish green calico printed fabric that my mother had been wearing on a day when I was whipped for whatever reason. I can feel the lingering sting of the leather belt as I rubbed at what I believed were the welts on my bare legs. Truthfully, I can't remember why I earned the belt. Tears were still wet on my cheeks from the crying I had done after receiving the whacks with the belt.

I touched the quilt on the yellowish green calico

printed spot and it felt damp from the tears I must have shed in my sleep.

When I climbed from my bed, I looked in the bathroom mirror and noticed my red swollen eyes.

"Is the quilt doing this to you?" I asked my reflection.

Of course, my response was going to be no, it couldn't be doing anything to me. The quilt was a thing. It had no life.

CHAPTER 4

SALT AND PEPPER

A few days later, as I drove home from work, I saw a little girl walking along the side of the road and clutched in her hands were two little kittens. One was coal black, the other was snow white. Those two little creatures reminded me of Salt and Pepper.

I went to bed that evening with the images of Salt and Pepper firmly planted in my mind. It was no wonder that the unhappy events that surrounded the short lives of my two gorgeous cats invaded my dreams while I was covered by the quilt.

Pepper, of course, was black with the brightest yellow eyes I had ever seen. He was a loving kitten who never got the chance to grow into an adult cat because he died a death of the unknown. I found him dead next to the house. He had no mark of violence or blood. My thought was that he ate some rat poison that the neighbors had put along the creek behind the house to kill off the multiplying rat population. Pepper's death was not so hard to take because he really looked like he died peacefully without a struggle. I shed some tears for him but I was glad his death was gentle.

Salt was not so lucky.

It was Saturday. There was no school and really no reason to get up early except for the fact that I slept in the living room on the sofa bed which meant that I had to get up early no matter what day of the week it was.

I looked out of the living room window across the road about half way up the driveway that climbed the hillside to a neighbor's house. My eyes caught a streak of white as Salt came running down the hill as if something were chasing him. Behind the white blur came a black blur and I immediately knew that the neighbor's dog had slipped his chain and was chasing my cat trying to catch him for the kill.

I ran to the door and reached the front porch just in time to see the pick-up truck hit Salt flipping him into the air throwing him into the weeds on the side of the road.

The pick-up truck kept going especially after the driver saw that I was a witness. The dog tucked its tail and scampered back up the driveway. I took off running to help Salt.

I found him in the tall weeds by following the cries of

the wounded animal pleading for help. When I reached him he was moving around, just barely. I picked him up, cradled him, and ran back to the house where I looked to my dad for help.

I held Salt while dad drove as fast as he could to get to the vet's office.

The vet poked and prodded on my cat before giving him a shot supposedly for pain. He then told me I could take him home, that he would be fine in a couple of days.

Dad paid the man for what little he had done and I held onto my cat as we drove home.

"Ellen, take the cat out to the building and sit with him for a while. I'll send your brother out with some old rags for the cat to sleep on and to keep him warm."

"Is he going to live, dad?" I asked tearfully.

"I don't know," he said sadly as he walked toward the house.

In my heart I knew the answer to that question.

Lee came running out with some rags which were made of mom's old faded dresses that were thread bare in places and had been washed of all of their bright colors. The faded yellows, greens, reds, and blue in a multitude of designs were piled in a heap so I could share them with the cat.

"That cat's going to die," shouted my brother in an ugly teasing tone.

"I know. But until he does, I'm going to stay with him," I snapped back softly so as not to disturb my feline patient with my loud voice.

I sat with my cat, my beautiful white Salt, and patted his head and loved him the best I could all evening.

Salt tried to get up but his back was broken. I could see that. Why hadn't the vet seen it? I wondered why he had told me Salt would be all right in a couple of days? I knew the cat was going to die. I knew it wouldn't be very long until that happened.

"Ellen, come in for supper," said dad as he entered the building where I was sitting on the old faded dresses on the concrete floor.

"Ask mom to save me some, okay?"

Dad shook his head and left. He let me suffer with my dying cat.

I rubbed Salt's head and talked to him cooing to him like one would try to soothe an infant. He didn't cry like he was in pain. It was more from the frustration of not being able to rise up and walk.

I didn't turn on the light in the building. I sat across from the only window with Salt in the darkness inside the small room of a building and stared into the skies where the stars were flickering brightly around the small slice of the moon.

Salt's breathing was beginning to slow and he was making no more effort to move. My beloved cat finally died as I held him on my lap.

I cried until I couldn't cry anymore. I tried to make Salt comfortable on the pile of old dresses knowing full well that it wasn't comfort for the cat that I was after.

"Dad, Salt is dead," I said upon entering the house.

"Go eat your supper," he said as he turned his head quickly from me so I wouldn't see the tears glistening in his eyes.

When I awoke from the sadness that had infiltrated my mind, I saw the quilt bunched up on the corner of my bed with the area depressed in the center looking as if my cat had been using the quilt for a bed.

"Oh, Salt, what a horrible way to die," I mumbled as I walked to the bathroom to get my day started.

It seemed up to this point, most of my dreams or nightmares had been about my mother which, I guess, is understandable since most of the quilt was made up of her leftovers from making her own dresses. Not all of the fabric pieces were exclusively mom's.

I took the quilt off the bed for the summer. My mind needed a rest and the quilt was a little too heavy for comfortable sleeping.

CHAPTER 5

HE TOUCHED ME

When fall arrived, the quilt returned to cover my bed like a bedspread. I loved the beauty of the handmade quilt but I hoped the dreams and nightmares would not return.

The first night of the return of the quilt was peaceful with only one memorable dream and definitely no frightening nightmares.

A bright square of white was what incited the memory the second night. The same white of grandpa's hair and dress shirt he wore each and every Sunday.

I had just completed the second grade which made me six years old. It was summer vacation and we were visiting my grandfather on my dad's side of the family.

Grandpa Hudson had snow-white hair and a lot of it

considering his age, which was somewhere in the early seventies.

He was a tall man; the only tall man I can ever remember seeing in dad's family.

Grandpa was angular, meaning that his bones and joints did not curve softly. They seemed to operate in distinct angles like ninety degrees and forty-five degrees,

He was slender and old age handsome.

I liked Grandpa Hudson because he was soft spoken and had eyes that smiled with the happiness that curved his mouth gently.

I heard my daddy tell someone, I can't remember who, that Grandpa Hudson used to be a mean one when he was young and that he got into a lot of trouble of his own making. There was nothing about Grandpa Hudson that would tell me he was ever the way my daddy said except maybe his sparkling eyes. Those bright blue eyes hid a lot of secrets behind the sparkles.

Grandma Hudson was the picture of a grandmother. She was short and round. She had salt and pepper gray hair and golden, wire-rimmed glasses that were perched on her tiny nose. Everybody that knows both of us tell me that I am just like my Grandma Hudson. I hope so.

When we visited Grandpa and Grandma Hudson it was always a short, whirlwind visit so I really didn't get to know them very well. The visits to their house that was located on a river bank nestled in the mountains happened once a year at the most.

Quilted Memories

I had finished the first grade which I had gleefully passed.

"Ellen, what's wrong with your knee?" Grandpa Hudson asked with a concerned look on his face.

"Daddy says I have warts."

"Have you been playing with any frogs?"

"My teacher told me you don't get warts from frogs."

"Okay then, have you been playing in the creek out behind your house?"

I looked at Grandpa Hudson and saw that he was smiling, so I answered truthfully.

"Yes, but don't tell on me."

"You probably got the warts from the water where the frogs live. Don't you think?"

"I guess so….Grandpa, how did you know we had a creek behind our house."

"Don't know. It just came to me that you played in the creek."

I reached down and rubbed at the ugly warts.

"Come over here and sit on my lap."

I ran to him happily and climbed onto his knee. I hugged him tight to let him know how much I loved him.

Grandpa Hudson reached around me and put both of

his hands on my knee. Then he bowed his head and got real quiet.

I didn't say anything. I knew that he was praying as he held his hands on my knee.

It felt hot where his hands were touching, but not too hot.

I watched his lips move as he prayed. I could feel his warm, gentle breath being pushed from his mouth by his prayer words. He held his eyes closed and the grimace on his face made him look as if he were in pain.

Even though I was only six years old, I sat silently. Mommy had taught me not to interrupt people, especially old people, when they were praying. She said God didn't like it when I did that.

"Dad, what are you doing?" shouted my daddy to grandpa.

"Praying for Ellen. Healing her warts."

"Don't do that. You know I don't believe in that crap."

Grandpa Hudson moved his hands from my knee and daddy walked on to the house glancing back at grandpa and me before he walked through the doorway.

"Ellen, when you wake up tomorrow one of the warts will be gone. The second one will disappear next week. You won't even feel it when it happens. Now, let's go inside and see what everyone else is doing."

I never thought anymore about what Grandpa Hudson

had done until I went to wash up the next morning.

Mommy filled up an old metal washtub telling me to strip down and climb into the warm water first before my brother, who was always boy dirty, got his chance at the clean water.

Mommy scrubbed at me like she was in a hurry to get this chore over and done with. It was a task she hated because there were no bathrooms in the house. She had to draw the water from the well, bucket after bucket full. Carry some of the water over to the wood cook stove where she would pour it from the bucket into a big metal pot and heat it to almost boiling. Then she would have to carry the big hot pot of water outside to the wash tub.

She pulled on my leg and stretched it out of the water in front of me.

"One of your warts is gone, Ellen."

I looked at my knee and she was right. Grandpa Hudson had told me it would be gone but I had forgotten about it.

When we said goodbye so we could get back home on a drive that would take us three hundred miles away, Grandpa Hudson looked at my knee because it extended passed my shorts.

Grandpa Hudson winked at me and I tried to wink back at him. I wasn't very good at winking. I ended up squinching up both eyes and actually holding one of them closed so I could see with the other eye.

I didn't tell daddy the wart disappeared just like Grandpa Hudson said it would.

When school started the next week, I was a proud second grader with a full year of experience under my belt.

I wore a short dress to school and my knee with the one wart was displayed for all to see.

When we went to recess, I joined the group of girls who were jumping rope.

When my turn came to jump I managed to get my feet tangled into the turning rope and down I went landing on my knees.

I expected to have some really bloody cuts and scratches scraped into the skin that covered my knees. When I stood up, both knees were not scraped and the wart was gone.

I rubbed my hands against both my knees just to be sure there wasn't anything there. On the knee where the wart had been, I could still feel the heat from Grandpa Hudson's hands.

I smiled when I realized that Grandpa Hudson's laying on of hands had taken away the warts.

I never told my daddy about it. As a matter of fact, this is the first time I've ever told anyone about it.

I wish Grandpa Hudson were alive today so he could read this story to the world.

Just to let you know, my daddy did believe in God. He

just couldn't believe that the mean man Grandpa Hudson used to be could be the same man with the God-given power to heal with his hands.

The second night didn't prove to be as restful.

I was wearing the old hand-me-down navy blue dress that my neighbor had given me. I was so proud to wear it because it wasn't homemade and it actually had some style. Not the current style of the day, of course, but the older fad-gone-bad style that told the world that my mom didn't make the dress.

I was walking along Route 139 on my way to Twin Valley Hollow Road when a man, who appeared to be working on the side rails of the bridge I had to cross, spoke to me.

"Little lady, how are you?" said the smiling man as he stood up straight resting his back from the task he had been performing.

I smiled in return and walked closer to see what he had to say.

We lived in a rural area where there were no strangers. It was surely a surprise to see a person I didn't know. I wasn't the least bit afraid of him. I had no reason to be afraid of him. I was friendly with everyone because I knew no strangers.

"Fine," I answered. "My name is Ellen. Who are you?"

"Johnny is my name, little lady. Come here and shake hands with me. It is so nice to meet a sweet young thing like you."

I walked closer and he grabbed me. I felt his arm go around me in a sweaty hug. I returned the hug quickly so I could back away from him.

Then I felt his other arm reach up under my dress and he put his hand on my private spot. His finger pressed up hard where he shouldn't have been touching me. I wriggled around and got loose from his grasp.

He was still smiling and talking friendly like.

I stood with my mouth open looking at him. I didn't know what he was trying to do but I didn't think he should be doing it.

I backed away from him and skirted my way around him to get past him on my way to visit my girlfriend, Linda, who lived almost to the end of that road.

I was only seven and I was afraid to tell anybody what the man had done because I wanted to be able to walk to my girlfriend's house again. If daddy found out about the strange man and where he put his hand, I wouldn't be allowed to walk anywhere alone. I would have to have my older brother with me and I surely didn't want that to happen all the time.

When I awoke from my memory, I found I had pulled the quilt up between my legs. Perhaps I was trying to protect myself. Whatever the reason, it was very uncomfortable.

CHAPTER 6

TRICK OR TREAT

Several nights hurried by before I returned to the land of strange dreams.

"Mom, can I go trick or treating?"

"You know your daddy doesn't want you and Lee to do that."

"I know, but daddy isn't here and all my friends are going. Can't I go?"

I knew my brother had already asked and she had said no, but I thought I would try again. Mommy usually wasn't as mean as daddy. Sometimes she would let us do things as long as we didn't tell daddy about it.

"Who's going?"

"Kathy, Vicky, Carol, and me, if you let me."

"What are you going to dress up in?"

"Have you got an old sheet?"

"Yes."

"I'll go as a ghost. Lee can dress up like a hobo and go with his buddies."

"Your daddy will be mad."

"We won't tell him. Please, Mom, let us go?"

"I don't know…"

"Why won't he let us go trick or treating anyway?"

"He looks at it as charity and only poor people go out begging."

"Everybody goes begging, not just poor people. Any way we are poor, aren't we?"

"Yes, but your daddy doesn't want charity."

"It's fun, mommy. I don't know what charity is but if trick or treating is charity, then I like it."

"Okay, okay, but your daddy better not find out."

Lee was dressed in some of daddy's raggedy old work clothes that were somewhat holey but we made them worse by tugging new holes into them. We blacked his face with some coal dust and gave him a potato sack in which to carry his candy.

I got the old white bed sheet that we cut in a round circle so it wouldn't drag the ground. Two holes were cut out for the eyes and I edged them with black to make them more noticeable. I tied a small rope loosely around my neck to hold the sheet in place. By the time we were finished with our costumes it was almost dark.

Lee took off to go meet his buddies. He was three years older than me so he didn't want me tagging along to embarrass him.

I ran next door to Kathy's house and stood on the porch waiting for her to come outside. I waited and waited for what seemed forever until her mother finally came to the door when some other trick or treaters rang the doorbell.

"Mrs. Groves, is Kathy here? I've been waiting out here like she told me."

"No, Ellen, she and the other two girls, Vicky and Carol, went trick or treating in Rosemount. Were you supposed to go with them?"

"Yes ma'am," I said as I tried to stifle the tears. "They must have forgotten about me."

I took off running by myself. I was going to go door to door alone. I wasn't going to miss Halloween Beggars Night.

We lived in a rural area where the houses were built in clusters. Once you knocked on the doors of the houses in each cluster, you had to walk a long distance to get to another cluster of houses.

Most people had their porch lights turned on brightly. The houses with brightly shining porch lights were the only houses I wanted to visit.

The walk between the clusters of houses was scary because there were no lights of any kind lighting the way. Only the full moon shining above my head offered any illumination. The twinkling stars seemed to be too far away to be of any help.

I tried to keep my eyes focused straight ahead of me so that I wouldn't trip on anything in the darkness. Besides, the shadows along the side of the road seemed to move when I watched them and that was making me even more scared than I already was.

It wasn't nice of Kathy, Carol, and Vicky to go off and leave me, but it had happened before on several occasions. I tried, I mean I really tried, to fit in but they wouldn't let me. I was an outsider and would always remain an outsider and I really didn't understand why.

I was getting tired and I was too far from home to slow down. I had to keep walking to get myself home before it was too late and then mommy would get mad at me. She was going to be mad at me if she found out I had gone out at night alone. I wasn't going to tell her and I hoped Lee wouldn't find out and tell her.

The cars were few and far between so I didn't have to worry about getting hit along the side of the road. The trees off to the side held the darkness beneath them hiding anyone or anything that was waiting in that darkness.

"Wooooooooo!" came a wavering shout from my right side off into the darkness.

I looked towards the sound but saw nothing. My eyes were wide-open as I tried to see through the darkness.

"Wooooooooo!" came the sound again as I hurried my pace along towards home.

I was scared. I took off running as fast as my little short fat legs could carry me.

I had to stop to catch my breath. I looked around as I tried to silence my breathing. I heard footsteps slapping against the pavement behind me.

"Woooooooo! Woooooooo! Woooooooo!" chorused several voices of which one sounded very familiar.

"Lee! Is that you chasing me?" I screamed as I stopped dead in my tracks.

Suddenly whoops of laughter swirled up from behind me and I knew my answer.

I stood and waited for them to catch up with me. I was tired of being alone and scared.

"I thought you were going with Kathy and the others? Where are they?"

"They went on ahead. I had to sit a spell and rest and they didn't want to wait for me," I lied hoping he wouldn't find out the truth.

"Well, we'll walk you home but I'm not ready to go in yet. Tell mom I'll be at Lonnie's house and I'll be home in about an hour."

"She'll be mad."

"That's okay. She'll get over it," he said in a smart-alecky way.

Mommy was mad and she was waiting for me to get home. It seemed that Kathy's mother made Kathy come by the house to tell mommy and me how sorry she was for forgetting about me. Mommy knew I had been alone when I went trick or treating.

She whipped me with a switch when I walked through the front door. She whipped me again when I told her what Lee had told me to tell her. She waited by the door and whipped Lee as soon as he got home.

Trick or treating wasn't fun anymore.

I woke up from my restless sleep and discovered that my quilt was turned bottom side up on my bed. The white sheet that had been used as the backing for the quilt was now on the top reminding me of the sheet I had thrown over my head when I went trick or treating.

I frowned at the memory because getting a whipping wasn't fun. But getting two whippings for something that wasn't my fault was no fun at all.

Trick or treating and Halloween reminded me that the world was filled with witches. They might not all ride on brooms but they were present in various shapes and sizes representing good and evil.

Linda was good. Linda was always a little different.

"How are you doing, Linda?" I asked each time I walked passed her.

"Fine," was always her one word response. We never did get into any prolonged conversation. I don't know why. It just happened that way.

I met Linda Snider in high school. She was always a little different from the other girls in our classes. I guess that little bit of difference is what drew me, wanting me to enter her sphere of friendship. The daily salutations caused me to believe that Linda and I were friends.

I was always an outsider mainly because I didn't have the money to buy myself the necessary popular friends that would pull me into the correct circles. I observed in my school that the most popular girls had something to give to others such as candy, make-up, secrets, and the like. Some had even given themselves to the boys who were attracted to them like flies to honey.

I guess that lack of money, lack of willingness to get into the back seat of a car, and lack of popularity led me to form friendships with others who were out of the loop.

Linda was a plain girl in that she had no outstanding features that would cause you to think she could win a beauty contest.

She had long brown hair, sort of a medium shade of

mousy brown that curled naturally a little too much to be in style.

She covered her brown eyes with glasses that were made with plastic frames of a neutral bland color. The lenses enlarged her eyes a bit giving her an off balance look.

She dressed in well-worn clothes that were best suited for an older woman. The skirts were a little too long and the blouses were a little too big causing the shoulder seam to drop down her arm a bit.

When I looked at Linda Snider, I knew she was just a bit out of step with the rest of the flighty females. That made her just like me.

Linda Snider tended to fade into the woodwork of any room in which she was standing, but I always knew she was there. There was something about her that imprinted her presence into my mind.

We were never close friends or best friends, but we did acknowledge the existence of one another. We were friends.

"What are you planning to do after graduation?" I asked Linda one day when I saw her standing in line awaiting her turn to practice receiving her diploma.

"Nothing in particular. Maybe get married. Have a bunch of kids. Further my religious studies. What about you?"

"I can't afford to go to college. I'll just try to find a job and do what every other woman does. Get married and have kids, I guess."

At that time my name was called and I had to walk away but I wanted to know what religious studies Linda was talking about. I really hadn't known she was religious. Actually I thought she didn't attend any church at all.

After high school graduation everyone drifted away into the challenge of a new life and new beginnings.

I had married and given birth to my eldest son before I gravitated into Linda Snider's world once again.

We lived in an old, formerly ethnic neighborhood that was transitioning itself into a slum with absentee landlords who owned run down houses and apartment buildings.

The color of the inhabitants was changing as the condition of the housing deteriorated. I'm not implying anything other than that was how things happened in that city. The pattern was always the same no matter what the neighborhood.

The white ethnic population moved out renting their long time family homes to white migrants from the southern states who were searching for an easier way of life that didn't include coal mining.

After a while the white migrants would become discouraged and would leave to return to their origins leaving behind them homes that suffered greatly from neglect.

The next wave of people that moved to the area would be Hispanic and the color change would flow from ethnic white and southern migrant white to light brown. The language changed from American English to Spanish of all dialects with a complete cultural difference.

Then the color would darken and the atmosphere would become dangerous making it a place to avoid at all costs. The area became a haven for those who had no other place to go and the living quarters reflected the desolation of the people living behind closed doors.

Homeless people and drug addicts were living in the rundown and condemned houses without any hope of climbing up that ladder to success.

I was still living in an area that had remained ethnic and white. It was a small island surrounded by change. The change was creeping in around the edges so I knew I would have to move soon for my own self-preservation as well as the protection of my family members.

I was walking through the city park located at the end of my street when I saw Linda Snider.

"Hi, how are you?" I asked a surprised Linda.

"Ellen, it that you? Ellen?"

"Yes, you remember me. It's good to see you, Linda. How are things?"

"Fine. I'm married now. I'm no longer Linda Snider. The last name is Walker."

"I'm married, too. I've gone from Ellen Hudson to Ellen Szklarz."

Quilted Memories

"Do you have any children?"

"Yes, a son named Eddy. How about you?"

"No, no children," Linda answered softly and sadly.

"I don't live very far from here. Why don't you come with me and I'll show you so we can visit again?"

"I can't today. I live on the next block over. It's the white house with the black shutters. You can't miss it. Stop by any time," Linda said as she hurried away from me.

Linda was dressed in white, almost like an old fashioned nursing nun. Her skirts were long, almost touching the ground and flowing. Perhaps she appeared more like an angel. That's it, her light flowing clothing was angelic in appearance.

Her long brown hair was reflecting sunlight making it seem like it was lighting up from inside the strands. The frames of her eyeglasses sparkled like diamonds not detracting in the least from her appearance.

Linda Snider was really different.

The next day I decided to walk to Linda's house. My mother who lived next door to me was watching my napping son so I had a few free moments.

I found the white house with the black shutters. The white of the paint took on a glow that no other house on the street possessed. The black shutters were decorated with circled stars that were also black. The stars seemed to be raised from the surface of the shutters. It was very impressive and the only house on the street that was not suffering from neglect.

Before my knuckles were able to rap on the red door, Linda opened it and asked me to enter.

"I knew you would come by today. I'm glad you have thought enough of me to want to visit."

I didn't know how to respond to such a greeting.

"Please sit down, won't you?"

"What a lovely room," I said as I looked around me.

The room was white, completely white. The sofa, chairs, draperies, throw pillows, everything was spotlessly white.

"Thank you, Ellen."

"How do you keep it so clean?"

"My husband and I are the only ones who live here. We rarely have company. It really is no problem to keep clean. Would you like to see the rest of the house?"

"Sure," I said as I stood up to be led on a tour.

She took me to the kitchen that looked normal except that everything that could be white was. The bedroom was much the same way. Everywhere there was white.

The last room I toured was the one that interested me most. It was the altar room.

The altar room had no windows and the only light

within the walls was coming from the candles that were flickering on a pedestal that Linda explained to me was that of her altar. One of the candles was burning brightly covered by a red glass globe spraying red everywhere the white would have been.

Hanging nearby on a hook was a white hooded robe with no adornments other than the white rope cinch that was hanging loosely at the sides.

On the altar were a container of salt, some incense, ceremonial knives, a large book, and a cassette recorder with tapes next to it.

"What kind of knives are those."

"Actually they are merely kitchen utensils that are used solely for my altar now."

"What do you use them for?"

"Some of the rituals I follow require the use of sharp instruments."

On the floor I saw what looked like a faint trace of a circle of something that had been dropped onto the floor.

"What about the ring on the floor?"

"That's my protective circle. It is made of salt, sea salt when I can get it. When I'm within that circle no harm will come to me. That's also the reason I have a red door. It is to scare away any unwanted demons."

My mouth must have been hanging open in total surprise.

"Didn't you know I was a witch?" she asked me as she smiled sweetly.

"No, I had no idea," I stammered in return.

"I thought that was why you wanted to visit me. I thought maybe you were seeking help with your personal problems. I know you have been having marriage problems."

I looked at her and frowned.

"How do you know I'm having problems?"

"I'm a witch."

"What kind of witch?"

"I am a white witch. I practice good magic. I help people."

"Linda, the only reason I came to see you was to renew an old friendship. I have no intention of asking you for help of any kind, magic or otherwise."

"Yes, I know that, Ellen. I just wanted you to know that my services are available."

"To do what?"

"Whatever you think will help you."

"Well, that's not what I'm after. I just wanted a friend."

We returned to the living room and I said goodbye. I never visited Linda Snider Walker again. I've often wondered how she has survived in a world that totally condemns the pagan religion that she practices.

Perhaps I should have gotten some magical help from Linda. Maybe I wouldn't have had to endure two bad marriages before I finally arrived at the good one. Maybe my eldest son wouldn't have been hit by a car and maybe my youngest son wouldn't have moved to Nebraska, so very far away.

I always knew Linda was a little different. I just didn't know how different until I visited her and saw it with my own eyes.

I'm so very proud to say that Linda Snider Walker was and is my friend, I hope. It really wouldn't hurt to know a good witch.

CHAPTER 7

THE DRAGON GREW AND GREW

My mind films continued to project themselves into my being. This film was prompted into life by the purple square that shimmered like the prehistoric dawns that have been portrayed in the movies.

The dragon opened its mouth and yawned, consciously letting the moonlight glint off the razor sharp teeth.

I was supposed to be impressed.

Suddenly the creature pulled its head back with its long muscular neck and started snapping its teeth looking as if it were chewing on a tough piece of air. The strength of the jaws caused the snapping to sound like grinding clashes of enamel coated spears.

Quilted Memories

Now, I was impressed.

I tried to back away, move quickly; but something was holding me back. I struggled with my restraints knowing that my real danger was in front of me pulling its head back and suddenly shoving it forward opening and closing its gigantic mouth inches from my face.

I couldn't focus on what was holding me, keeping me from running because I was dodging my head front and back, side to side, trying to stay away from the snapping teeth. I wildly swung at the dragon knowing full well that if I, by chance, happened to hit the creature it wasn't going to matter because the blows would not phase it.

The dragon continued to come at me, lunge at me, snapping, gnashing, but suddenly I realized it wasn't reaching me. It, too, was being prevented from actually grabbing hold of my body and ripping me to shreds spreading blood and gore throughout the room with its razor sharp teeth.

Even though my brain assessed the fact that the dragon wasn't going to be able to reach me, my body was telling me to get out of there. Yet, I couldn't break myself free from the grasp of something or someone that was holding me back, preventing me from running.

I struggled and fought, not the dragon, but my captor.

"Let me go," I begged as I thrashed around flailing my arms and kicking my feet.

I heard nothing except my own pleading. There was no heavy breathing, no loud yelling or screaming telling me to stop.

"Why don't you let me go?"

"Ellen, are you all right?" said a voice from the other side of the door.

"What?" I asked as I tried to figure out what was happening.

"You were screaming and talking in your sleep. Are you all right?" asked Betsy my good friend and housemate.

"Oh, yeah, sure, I'm fine. Just had a bad dream. That's all. A bad dream, Betsy. Go back to bed," I whispered so I wouldn't wake up the rest of the sleeping household.

"Do you need anything?"

"No, nothing, just go back to bed."

I reached for my lamp on the table next to my bed and flooded my room with light so I could see what had been holding me back.

I found nothing that would hold me in place unless it was my bedclothes that were wrapped around me bunched up at my waist.

I touched my brow and discovered the cold sweat of fear and my heart was racing trying to run out of my chest. I took a couple of slow, deep breaths as I tried to slow down the blood pounding though my veins.

Glancing at the clock, I saw that it was three o'clock in the morning. I had three more hours remaining of the night until I had to get ready for work. I didn't want to return to the specter of the dragon so I picked up a book and started reading to quietly pass the time.

"What was your dream about?"

"Oh, nothing, I really can't remember it now," I answered with a lie. I didn't want to discuss it. The thought of the dragon with the glinting razor teeth made me shudder.

"It really had you going. Are you sure you can't remember any of it?"

"Betsy, I don't even want to think about it. If I can remember the dream, I'll tell you about it later, okay."

"Sure," said Betsy who wasn't convinced that I was speaking the truth.

This sudden onslaught of nightmares was upsetting me. I couldn't remember at any time in my life ever having a nightmare until the dragon started invading my dreams.

Why a dragon? Did that monster of a midnight menace represent something that was happening in my life? If so, who? Or What?

Maybe my life wasn't so great, but I was working on that.

I fought for and attained a divorce from a monstrous husband, the father of my two sons, so I knew that problem was eliminated. At least, I hoped it was eliminated. I never wanted to have to expose myself or my children to that kind of hell again.

My new life started with my friend, Betsy, and her three children moving into my home to help with the expenses for both of our broken families.

Then, I met Jack and I was happy. The idea that a man really liked me, wanted to be with me, and share moments of happiness with me was a new, wonderful feeling that I truly hoped would last forever.

"Let's go out tonight, Ellen," said Betsy the moment I arrived home from work.

"Did you get a chance to wash the laundry today?" I asked knowing that she hadn't done any of the household chores.

"No, I was busy."

"Doing what?"

"That's none of your business."

"Oh yes, it is my business. You haven't been pulling your full share of the load around here," I added angrily.

"I will just as soon as I find another job."

"When will that be? I need some help with the bills and buying food not to mention paying the rent."

"I'm looking, Ellen. That's what I was doing today."

"Really? Did you have any luck?" I said sarcastically.

"No, not yet."

"You could have started on the laundry when you got

back from looking for a job. By the way, who watched the kids while you were looking?"

"Stop this, Ellen. I don't need to go through the third degree every time you get home from work," said Betsy as she whirled around to leave the room.

This was almost like being married. The only difference was that there was no sex involved in this relationship. Betsy had her men and I had Jack.

I didn't go out. I chose to stay home and attack the mountain of laundry that was rising higher and higher in our oversized bathroom.

Betsy decided to cruise the bars alone. That was nothing new for her. She did that a lot, too much actually. I had heard rumors that she was loose and traveled in circles much different from mine, but I didn't want to believe them. I kept my blinders firmly in place so I wouldn't lose my friend.

I knew Jack wasn't going to be waiting for me at the TriBar because he was out of town. I stayed home to wash clothes and watch the five children that filled the house.

"Ellen, wake up. Ellen, I need to talk to you," said a tipsy Betsy when she arrived home after the bars had closed at 2:30 in the morning.

"What? What's wrong? Are the kids all right?" I asked as I opened my eyes wide to focus on the specter of a drunk Betsy wobbling at the side of my bed.

"He's married."

"Who's married? What are you talking about?"

"Jack is married."

"I know that. He and his wife are separated. He's getting a divorce."

"I don't think so."

"What do you mean?" I was wide awake now.

"He and his wife were playing kissy face when I went into the bar where you usually meet him. She is a red head, isn't she? I thought you said he was supposed to be out of town."

"That's what he told me. Are you sure it was Jack? And his wife?"

"Would it matter who it was. If he was playing kissy face with another woman?"

"I guess not."

"It was his wife. I asked Mike to make sure."

"Go on to bed, Betsy. I've got to work tomorrow. I've got to get some sleep."

I knew I was going to have a problem trying to make myself return to the deep sleep I had entered before Betsy so rudely interrupted me. Why she had to tell me about Jack in the middle of the night was beyond my comprehension. Unless, she wanted to see me get all bent out of shape. That didn't happen, or at least, I didn't let her see that happen. I didn't let her see the tears that flowed down my cheeks as I cried into my pillow.

Quilted Memories

Finally, I fell asleep.

The dragon grew and grew from a tiny speck to a looming monster as it overtook my sleeping mind. I could see its mouth opening to let me see the razor sharp teeth dripping with a red liquid.

Was that blood?

It opened its mouth wider so I could see the bloody, grisly, body part that was positioned on its tongue.

The body part was moving, pumping, forcing the blood to gush from the dragon's mouth.

The dragon didn't try to close its mouth. It wanted to flaunt its gory, bloody meal in front of me as it swung its head back and forth emitting a growl of sorts to make sure that I paid close attention.

I could do nothing but stare at the human heart that was pumping and pushing blood from the dragon's mouth.

I looked down at myself and noticed a hole, a big bloody hole, where my heart used to be.

I grabbed for my chest and in so doing I must have hit myself really hard because I woke up with a terror I had never known at any time in my life.

I had felt the pain, the wrenching of my heart from my body by those razor sharp, piercing teeth. Did I cry out? No one came running to pound on my bedroom door to demand my explanation. Was I having a heart attack? Was that the reason for the ripping of my heart from my chest?

My nightgown was soaked.

"Do I have blood on me? Is there something really wrong?" I asked myself those questions as I painfully struggled to reach for the lamp next to my bed.

The light blinded me when the knob was turned but I was relieved to see and feel the brightness fill the room and chase away the dragon.

My nightgown was not red with my blood nor was there a gaping hole in my chest where my heart had been removed. The wetness I had felt in the darkness was nothing but the sweat of fear and frustration.

"What are you trying to tell me?" I asked the four walls that surrounded me. "Who is the dragon? What is the dragon? Is someone trying to kill me? Please, tell me what I can do to stop this midnight torture?"

It was three in the morning and again I was afraid to return to the sleep I so very much needed.

I picked up my trusty reading material and tried to focus on the pages opened before my wide awake eyes. I read the first paragraph and it made no sense to me. I reread the same paragraph and slammed the novel closed.

Jack had filtered into my thoughts.

"He told me he was getting a divorce," I mumbled as I fought the tears of emotional pain that were building up behind my wide awake eyes. "I'm not going to cry."

I promised myself I would cry over no man ever again, not after the ugly divorce and evil words I had had to live through while I was fighting for the custody of my two sons. I had believed my husband when he told me he loved me after enduring the mental abuse he hurled at me daily.

"No man would ever want you. You're ugly. You're fat."

I wasn't ugly. I was overweight but I was working on that. It was a constant battle that I would have to fight for a lifetime. As far as no man ever wanting me was concerned, Jack wanted me. At least, I thought he did. Now, I'm not so sure.

"Why did Betsy get such pleasure out of telling me about seeing Jack and his wife, if she was his wife. Even if she wasn't his wife, why did she need to tell me about it? In the middle of the night?"

The work day was going to be long and I had plans to meet Jack at the bar as close to five o'clock as I could get there.

Concentration on the work at hand was difficult for me because so many thoughts and fears about my personal life kept shoving work related thoughts to the side.

"Hey, Ellen. Over here!" Jack shouted as I entered the very same bar where he and his wife were performing for Betsy and her entourage the previous night.

I acknowledged Jack with a nod and worked my way through the crowd to get to his side. Seeing Jack brought forth so many contradictions for me. The bittersweet fact that I loved Jack and I wanted so very much to be sitting next to him was trying to overpower my seething desire to slap his face.

"Where have you been? I thought you would be here earlier."

"Had to work over a little, but I'm here now," I answered as I tried to smile sweetly instead of plastering the judgmental smirk on my face.

"I saw Betsy last night. Did she tell you about it? How come you weren't with her?"

"Somebody had to do laundry. You told me you would be out of town."

"My plans changed. Maybe if you were here she would have acted more like you. You should have seen what she was doing. I don't believe you let her live with you and your kids."

"What are you talking about? What did she do?" I asked knowing full well that he was trying to divert the conversation away from what he was doing that same night.

"Well, everybody was buying her drinks and she was drinking them. She mumbled something about dumping her boyfriend and she was celebrating."

"Did you buy her a drink?"

"Sure I did, several as a matter of fact."

"What happened next?"

"She was getting silly, slap happy. Someone told her to

get on the table so he could see her dance. The crazy woman did. She climbed right on the table and started gyrating around, rolling her hips, doing sexy, come-on movements."

"And you guys let her. You kept stoking the fire by buying her more drinks."

"Then someone yelled "take it off" and that's exactly what she started doing until she got down to the bare skin. She kept right on dancing. She has a great body and now everybody knows it. That crowd in the place kept getting bigger and bigger while she was dancing."

"She had her clothes on when she told me about your wife and the love scenes you were acting out, right here in this same bar, probably right on these same two bar stools."

"Everyone handed her clothes back to her when the cops pulled up out front. She scooted off to the ladies' room, got dressed, and left. I guess that's when she went home. I think you should make her move out of your house. She's not a very good influence on you or your kids. Everybody will think you're just like her."

"Meaning what?"

"You're easy."

"Is that what you think?"

"I didn't say that."

"What about your wife, your red headed wife? Aren't you going to tell me about when your divorce is going to be final?"

"Now isn't the time, Ellen."

"When will it be the time, Jack?"

"I'll let you know."

"What gives you the right to tell me who can or cannot be my friend? You, the married man, who has been lying to me for months about getting a divorce from his wife."

"Ellen, we can't discuss this now."

"Fine, Jack. I'll see you," I said as I jumped from the bar stool and ran out the door.

I was driving home, alone, in the dark of night, fighting the desire and need to smash the car headlong into something to remove the pain I was feeling.

My best friend, Betsy, and my lover, Jack were at odds with each other but that wasn't the only battle going on in my mind. I knew I had to rid myself and my life of both Betsy and Jack because I didn't like what my future would be if either or both remained a part of it.

I didn't want to be like Betsy who would sleep with any willing male and enjoy it.

I didn't want to sit around as Jack's mistress waiting for the few moments he had to spare for me away from his wife and family. I was not a home wrecker. I fell in love with Jack but I didn't know there was a happy home to wreck. He lied to me and I accepted it.

The problems were growing and growing and they

were affairs of the heart.

I knew I had to solve those problems, starting the next day. I was going to eliminate Jack and Betsy from my life by forcing Betsy to move out of my home and by forcing Jack to move out of my heart.

It was late when I walked through my front door. I was quiet so I wouldn't bother the six sleeping bodies in the house. I tiptoed to my bedroom and fell across my bed fully clothed where I slipped into an exhaustion induced slumber.

A small speck of sparkly light filtered into the darkness of my dreamless sleep. I watched it grow and grow until the dragon was fully in front of my eyes.

The dragon did not open his mouth to threaten me with the moonlight glinting off of his razor sharp teeth. He did not sway in and out in a menacing manner as he roared.

I wasn't impressed.

CHAPTER 8

THE CHOIR

There were a few black cotton squares on the quilt that I tried so hard not to focus on in my mind or with my eyes. My dreams zeroed in on the black squares as if they were a mission of great importance.

Not being accepted in this little town because we were outsiders that had invaded them by moving into the area from another state, it was difficult for me to form any lasting long time friendships.

I wanted to belong, to be a part of the world of school that I was living in so I joined the choir. I loved to sing. Singing made me feel like floating on the notes to happiness and acceptance.

I would sing solos at church every chance I got. The preacher and his wife would take me with them when they went to visit the elderly in nursing homes where I would stand up and sing proudly for my captive audience. Those people didn't seem to care whether or not I was an outsider or that I was short and fat.

Quilted Memories

At school we practiced really hard for about a month because we were going to all climb aboard a school bus and go to a competition that would take place in the next county. The girls had to be dressed in black skirts and white blouses and the boys had to wear black trousers and white shirts.

The requirement for the black skirt and white blouse was a problem but mom and I found a solution in no time. We took one of the dad's shirts and revamped it to look more like a white blouse. Mom had some black fabric that she had never used for herself so she and I sewed up a black skirt.

The day of the trip aboard the school bus arrived. I was so excited. It never occurred to me that someone would have to drive me to the school. It was Saturday and the school bus didn't run its regular route to pick us up for our daily classes.

Dad was supposed to come home for the weekend but he had car trouble so he had to stay where he was. I had no way to get to the school.

I was crying as the cars drove by on the road in front of my house while I sat on the porch in my makeshift required choir clothes.

I spent hours on that front porch regretting the day I was born.

The background of the dreams was black. My skirt was black so all I could see was my head, arms and vivid white shirt that had been made into a blouse. I could see the river of tears rolling down my cheeks forming the ever-rising puddle of water at what should have been my feet.

I awoke with my quilt covering only my feet. The black squares seemed to be fluorescent and dancing on the quilt.

Why was I reliving all of the bad times in my life?

CHAPTER 9

THE NIGHT WALK

Spring was bursting out all around me and I knew I would soon be taking the quilt off my bed for the summer.

The calico patches filled with endless flowers represented the choice for dress fabric for my mother's homemade wardrobe.

My memories were being prodded forward to be noted before the quilt was removed.

What woke me up?

Did I hear something?

I sat straight up in bed as I strained to hear sounds that weren't familiar to me.

Was that a footstep? A board creaking? Heavy breathing?

Oh, how I hated trying to sleep in a place that wasn't my everyday home and hearth.

A slight breeze hit my frightened face. It seemed as though a door had been opened and closed quickly causing the disturbance of the air.

Perspiration was beading on my brow as I concentrated so hard on identifying the reason for my sudden awakening.

My eyes were open wide and blinking only when it became necessary.

My hearing was being impeded by the pounding of my heart in my chest.

I took a deep breath as quietly as I could so I wouldn't disturb the night visitor that was causing my sleep disruption.

Slowly I expelled the air I held in my lungs as I stared wide-eyed into darkness.

If I could see an outline, a form, something that would tell me what was lurking in the shadows planning to cause me harm.

Should I get out of bed and make a run for it?

I didn't know where my night visitor was standing. I would probably run into him in trying to escape.

Is anyone really there?

"Who's there?" I whispered softly.

No answer, no sound, nothing was forthcoming.

I turned my head from side to side trying to survey the

darkness, trying to see something, anything that would give me a clue.

I slid my left hand under the covers slowly. I wanted to suddenly whip the covers off of me and spring from the bed as fast as possible.

I felt a slight puff of air.

Where is that coming from? What is that?

I glanced toward the direction from where I thought the breeze was originating.

The window is slightly open. It's only a little breeze from outside.

That small discovery seemed to explain everything as far as my frightened mind was concerned.

I reached to the nightstand and pressed the switch on the lamp. The light was bright as it illuminated every dark corner of the room.

"Ellen, you're silly," I mumbled to myself. "You're visiting your Uncle Jim. No one would harm you. There is no reason for anyone to harm you. No reason at all," I said as I tried to reassure myself that I was acting like a child.

I was sleeping in the old farmhouse that was well over a hundred years old. It had many reasons to make noises. Parts had been literally falling off of the house for years and years because my Uncle Jim wasn't much for keeping up appearances.

"Go back to sleep," I said softly so I could hear the

sound of my own voice and nothing else.

The dreams started rolling in full vivid brighter than life color.

I was running.

The tall weeds were hitting my face. I was extending my arms in front of me and moving them to each side as if I were blind. I was trying to feel my way through the tall weeds but I couldn't see.

Why can't I see?

I could feel the moon shining over my head but I couldn't see it.

Why can't I see the moon? How do I know it's there if I can't see it?

Running further and deeper into the weeds I could feel the slap of the branches and leaves against my face. I had to continue to run. I had to get there. I had no other choice than to run to that tiny little one room house sitting on the hillside.

The house seemed to be moving further and further away from me.

"Why are you doing this?" I shouted. "Stand still, please. Don't move anymore. No, no please. Stay there."

I knew I was going to arrive at the one-room house too late. It would be all over before my foot would step across the threshold.

"Wait, please, don't move!" I shouted.

Quilted Memories

It was over.

My dream had ended and I shouted myself awake.

I glanced around me not realizing that my own shouts had pulled me from my dreams.

I reached for the lamp at my bedside so I could light up the room, every corner of the strange room, to check to see if someone had entered.

The light flooded the room and my eyes were drawn to the window that was slightly open. I knew I had to close that window or I would never be able to go back to sleep.

I climbed from my bed and tiptoed to the window where I pulled at the shade from the side so I could peek outside to view the isolated area surrounding the old farmhouse.

There were no outside lights, only the moon offered illumination. Nothing was stirring; no movements were being made by anyone or anything that my human eyes could see.

There were so many darker areas where the illumination of the moon could not penetrate to offer some hint of what was waiting in the murky blackness.

I let the shade fall softly back into place against the window.

"God, I wish I didn't have to go out there," I prayed.

I reached for my shoes because I couldn't wear slippers. The grass and weeds would be wet and would only ruin a pair of cloth-like, lightweight slippers.

I wrapped a warm, chenille robe around me and cinched it at my waist to keep it in place.

The flashlight, where was the flashlight?

I had to have a flashlight. I wanted to be able to shine what meager light I had into every dark corner within my line of vision.

I had placed it on the nightstand when I went to bed. I knew it had been there.

I got down on my hands and knees to look under the bed.

That's probably what woke me up the first time. I must have knocked the flashlight off the nightstand when I was sleeping. When it hit the floor with a bang, that's probably when I woke up. I smiled at the logical explanation. I really was acting like a child because I was so scared.

I reached for the flashlight and grabbed it along with some dust bunnies that had multiplied under the bed.

I stood up and slid the switch forward to check the brightness of the flashlight.

Nothing, no light.

I banged on the flashlight a couple of times and noticed the flashing of brightness as it struggled to catch hold of the battery forcing the illumination through the clear plastic cover that protected the small bulb. One more bang and the light caught hold. I slid the switch to the off position and slid it back on just to make sure.

I opened the bedroom door slowly and peeked around the door facing checking to see if anyone was out in the hallway. I wanted to be quiet. I didn't want to wake up Uncle Jim.

I turned no lights on in the old house. I used the flashlight as I pointed its beam to the floor shining on the path that would lead me out of the back door.

The snap of the lock was like the sound of a gun going off in a confined area. I looked around me and saw nothing nor did I hear anything, no movement coming from the direction of Uncle Jim's room. I took a deep breath and tugged at the doorknob.

The squeak of the metal against metal of the hinges echoed around me.

Why doesn't he oil those hinges?

I answered that question with, why should he? He doesn't fix anything else in the old house. I decided to let the door stand open while I continued my trek to the great outdoors.

On the stoop outside the door, I stepped on something that squished beneath my feet. When I shined the flashlight on the spot where I had stepped, I realized I had squashed a snail.

"Yuck," I said as I held my foot up looking at the bottom of my shoe.

I stepped off the stoop and onto the grass where I swiped my foot back and forth to get the snail guts and slime off of my shoe.

I shined the beam of the flashlight around me quickly to see if there were any dangers out there waiting to grab me.

My mind flashed on something red, a flash of red that my eye must have seen. I whirled the flashlight back to where I thought I saw the red.

I saw a furry creature that was as frightened as I was, running away from me into the darkness. It looked like a stray dog. At least, I hoped it was a stray dog.

I had to press forward. I had to go to the little one-room house on the side of the hill. It was the same little, one-room house that had appeared in my dream.

The path was well worn but it was beyond the fenced in yard. The cattle that grazed on the hillside, the sheep that munched on the grass, and the old mean turkey gobbler that guarded the area outside the fenced yard, could be lying in wait to antagonize anyone who was not on her toes.

None of the creatures were within the sight line of the beam of the flashlight but I knew I had better hurry.

I shined the flashlight beam down to the ground. I certainly didn't want to step in a cow pile or brush up against a thistle plant.

When I reached the door of the little, one-room house, I was so relieved. I turned the wooden block that was holding the door closed and stepped inside the room into total darkness. My flashlight had chosen that very moment to extinguish itself.

"Oh no," I whispered as I banged the flashlight with my hand. There was a flash of light and total blackness again. I banged again as I tried to keep myself from panicking.

Now what was I going to do?

I reached for the door and tried to push it open far enough so that it would stay open wide without any help.

"There, that's enough light. The moon will let me see what I need to see," I said as I tried to convince myself that I wasn't scared to death.

I lowered my panties and pulled up my robe and gown as I proceeded to perform the duties required of the night walk under the light of the moon.

"When will he ever get an indoor bathroom?" I asked as I rose from my sitting position over one of the two holes in the outhouse.

I ran back to the safety of the house using only the moon to light my way.

Oh, how I hated that night walk by the light of the moon.

"Thank goodness there is a moon," I said as I fell back to sleep under the covers of the old bed in the safety of my room.

Linda Hudson Hoagland

CHAPTER 10

DEADLY BEAUTY

The mind movies were not going to stop. The old, faded flowery curtains that my mother had given to me were waving seductively in front of me. They suddenly became stiff, unable to move, as if frozen into place and the fabric appeared fresh and new like it was when mom first purchased the fabric.

The alarm buzzed. I set it to ring every couple of hours to make sure I was still living. Thankfully the radio was on a battery backup.

The phone was still dead. I knew it would be when I picked it up each and every time, but I continued to pick it up. I had to hear the silence so I could reassure myself that I had checked and that I really wasn't dreaming.

It was so cold.

I walked around the house trying to keep myself busy so I wouldn't think about what was happening. I picked up and carried several items back and forth between the rooms telling myself that it was necessary for me to see what it looked like when I placed this picture there, or maybe moved it over there.

It was too cold.

No one was stirring that I could see from my living room window. It had been hours since I noticed any movement of any kind. My window onto the world didn't allow me much space to spy on others because I was perched atop a hill in a house that would be totally missed by anyone driving along the road below.

How cold can the body get?

"I need to get a dusting cloth," I told myself loudly. "This window sill is a mess."

I hurried into the kitchen and yanked open the drawer beneath the sink where I stored the cleaning cloths.

I reached to turn off the dripping faucet.

"Stop it, Ellen. You've got to leave that water running," I said as I scolded myself with harsh sounding tones.

How long will it be before the water stops dripping?

I returned to the window that required the dusting. That's all I was going to do. Dust only, because my hands wouldn't be able to tolerate the water needed for a thorough wash down.

I glanced out the kitchen window and observed no

movement of any living, breathing creature on the wooded area that grew its way up the mountainside. The trees were covered with the pristine white of fresh fallen snow. The beauty of the scene was magnificent but the danger lurking beneath the unexcelled beauty was what kept me from venturing out the door to find help and freedom from this isolation that I had wanted so very much - until now.

"I asked for this. I wanted this. I wanted to be up and away from the bothersome rush of the everyday world. I wanted to be special. Well - I am special. I am alone. I am so totally scared," I said loudly to no one because I was alone, as I had wanted to be.

"Whooooo! Whoooo!" screamed the wind as it circled the house.

A crash, a shattering of glass.

"That must be upstairs," I shouted as I took off running to find the destruction.

Both upstairs bedrooms were intact, but I could feel the breeze of a fresh opening to the outside world.

I opened the door to the attic storage room and was nearly blown over by a gust of wind. A tree limb was protruding inside my window wedged solidly in place. The size of the limb was going to prevent me alone from dislodging it and pushing it back to the great outdoors where it belonged.

I closed the door and placed a rolled blanket in front of the crack between the door and the floor to prevent the wind gusts from whirling through the remainder of the house.

"Someone will check on me. Someone will wonder where I am," I said as I slowly descended the stairs to the first floor.

I picked up the phone again and heard silence.

I was getting tired, so tired.

I knew I had to keep moving but for the life of me I couldn't remember why?

I went back to my window to the world and looked out at the valley below that was snow covered and lifeless.

I could see the road at the bottom of the hill that was my front yard, but I had not seen a car driving by for hours. Of course, one or two could have driven past my window to the world without my knowledge while I was in other parts of the house. It wouldn't have mattered anyway, no one could see me wave and beg for help.

"I asked for this. God help me, I asked for this," I cried without tears.

I was afraid the cold wet tears would freeze to my face.

I glanced at the clock. It was four in the afternoon. It would be dark soon.

How many days ago had the ice hit?

I couldn't remember how many nights I had been trying to stay alive under the mounds of quilts and blankets I piled onto the sofa where I slept as I tried to stay warm.

The snow is leaving. Is it melting?

No, the cold winter wind was blowing the fine, powdery snow off of the ice-covered world outside my window.

The gleaming, sparkling, deadly ice covered trees, grass, gravel, porch steps, and car outside my window were beckoning me to try to leave my winter wonderland and go into the world of people, smiling, helpful, friendly, wonderful people who would welcome my intrusion into their world.

"I've got to get out of here," I mumbled as I shoved my feet into the boots that were sitting next to my front door.

I opened the door and looked at my front porch. It looked safe enough. I figured I could cross those few feet of ice-covered wood boards to get to the eight steps that led to the yard.

When I reached the steps, I saw that they were snow covered. That meant that the deadly ice was hiding itself beneath the powdery snow.

My front steps had no handrail to which I could hold for safety. I thought it would be better if I sat down on my bottom and scooted down the steps. I had pants on as well as tights and long underwear to pad my bottom from the cold.

Eight times I bounced my bottom from step to step until I reached the ice-coated grass on of the ground. My feet slid off the next step just before my bottom hit that step each time. So much ice hidden beneath the snow. No wonder there was no one moving about at the bottom of the hill. Cars wouldn't be able to travel along the snow hidden inches of ice.

When I attempted to stand up, my feet flew from beneath me and I hit the ground hard. I had to be careful. I would slide down that hill over the steep ravine that led to the road at the bottom if I wasn't careful.

I couldn't get back up. No amount of scrambling and trying to position myself on the snow-covered ice would allow me to lift my body up vertically. From my position on all fours, I looked at my front steps. I tried to crawl onto the first step and slipped back to the ground. I had no handrail to help pull me up the steps.

I was stuck.

I couldn't get back inside my house.

"What am I going to do now?"

"The back door. Get to the back door," I answered myself as I struggled back into my position of crawling on all fours.

Every inch of snow-covered dirt and grass that surrounded the front and right side of my house sloped downward toward the bottom of another slope that traveled several feet before leveling off for a bit then downward again to a deep ravine that was formed by eons of flowing water that poured out of the mountain side. Only the back and left sides of the house were jutted up against the mountainside with no dangerous ravine reaching out to grab me.

Unfortunately, to follow the shortest path to the back door I had to traverse across the most dangerous areas and pray that I didn't slip.

I crawled like an animal around my house until I reached my back door. My feet and hands slid with every forward movement. But, I made it.

Once inside, I located anything and everything that I could burn. I piled it up outside my back door and set it on fire with the matches I had located in a kitchen cabinet drawer.

My bonfire outside my back door was a dangerous thing to do, but it kept me alive and it kept me fed. I thawed some soup that I mixed with melted snow so I could eat and kept myself going until the sunshine melted some of the deadly ice that coated my isolated world.

When the ice melted, I packed up all of my meager belongings I had not burned and moved into an apartment building where I could share my existence with others. I no longer wanted the loneliness and solitude.

CHAPTER 11

THE OLD BIKE

Loneliness and solitude seemed to constantly dwell with me as my memories brought forth the reminders.

Lee had an old bicycle that he let me use because he had done some odd jobs and saved enough money to buy him a brand spanking new bike.

"Be careful with it, Ellen. I want to sell the bike and get some spending money. Don't be wrecking it," he admonished me daily when he saw me walking toward the outbuilding where I kept the bike at night to keep it from being stolen.

"Okay, okay, I'll be careful," was my repetitive reply.

Most of the time I rode alone on flat areas where the only speed you could build up was due to pedal power. I was afraid to ride down the paved hills that seemed to be on every roadway that I cruised. If I came to a hill I would get off the bike and walk beside it down the hill until I arrived at a less treacherous area for safer riding.

I said most of the time I rode on flat areas and walked the bike down hills. The one and only time I rode down the hill that I had to walk up and down every time I went to my girlfriend's house, was one memory that was invading my dreams.

I was wearing an old dress that my mother had made for me from a piece of fabric that was white in the background and had strange looking flowers printed on it that had beige petals with bright pink centers. It looked to be a summery fabric but it was actually heavier in weight than many of the dresses I wore in the winter. I didn't like the ugly flowers on the white background so I wore it to play in every chance I got hoping it would soon wear out and be tossed into the rag bag. Besides, the white background and the stupid looking flowers made my chubby body look even bigger.

I had been to Linda's house for a visit but she and her family were getting ready to go somewhere so I had to leave sooner than I expected. I was walking my way back up the hill when a couple of school mates went riding past me and didn't walk down the other side of the hill after they had reached the top.

"Chicken!" screamed Sandy as she saw me start to push the bike over the crest of the hill.

"Brrrack, brrarck, brrrack," her companion Mary shouted as she mimicked the sounds of a chicken to emphasize her point.

I turned red from head to toe and jumped onto my bike without a thought other than wanting to make them eat their words.

The speed was gradual but to me it seemed to build up really quick. I was scared. Speed kills and I knew that was my fate. I was going to be killed as I rolled down this hill.

I felt the breeze rushing against my face forcing me to squinch my eyes up to tiny slits. Speed didn't cause me the adrenaline rush of pleasurable excitement. Speed actually made my stomach churn itself into knots of pain and pressure. The adrenaline was pure acid.

I tried to apply the brakes by pressing back against the pedal. I guess I was going too fast for them to work properly.

I glanced down at my feet and when I looked up again I saw the back side of the car jutting out into the road. I pressed the pedal to try to stop the bike but it was too late.

My bicycle tire bounced off the back tire of the green car that was backing out of a driveway. I hadn't seen the car until it was already an obstruction in my path because some tall shrubbery hid the vehicle from my view.

Moments later the driver of the car was helping me get to my feet. The bounce had thrown me hard against the handle bars and very nearly into the creek that bordered the opposite side of the road.

"I'm all right," I said as I bit back the tears of shame.

"You should have stopped, young lady," scolded the driver.

"I couldn't. I didn't see you because of those bushes," I said defensively. "You need to cut those bushes down so this doesn't happen again."

"I won't be doing that. No, I won't be. You shouldn't be on that bike if you don't know how to ride it."

I wasn't going to say another word. I clammed up and limped my way over to my banged up bicycle. I jerked it up and discovered that the wheels would not spin. The bike was so jammed up that there was no free movement anywhere on it.

There was absolutely no damage to the car. All I saw was a black blur on the white sidewall tire.

I laid the bike back down on the side of the road and limped my way through the short cut that went up Mr. Siler's driveway, where I crawled passed his garage on a narrow path that precariously bordered the edge of the creek bank. I followed the path through the garden across the creek from our house where I went in the back door and ran to the bathroom to clean the blood off my legs and check for any other damage I might have pounded onto my body.

I located the source of my limp. I had hit the handle bar so hard that a deep, dark ugly bruise was already forming on my inner thigh. It was a wonder that I hadn't broken every bone in my body and, at that point in time, I wasn't sure if I hadn't broken any bones.

I cleaned the cuts and scrapes and left them exposed to the air to heal. At least, they weren't bleeding any more.

"Ellen, where's my bike?" asked Lee when he saw me and the damage I had done to my body that was showing where the dress wasn't covering it.

"Up the road, in front of the Smith house on the creek bank. You'll have to go get it. I couldn't get it here by myself."

"What did you do to it?" he screamed at me.

"My front tire hit the rear tire of a car that was backing out of a driveway."

"Why didn't you stop?"

"I didn't see the car until it was too late to stop," I said as I fought back the wave of tears rising in my throat.

Lee took off running and came back about a half an hour later dragging the bicycle. It was damaged beyond repair. He was mad at me and I was, once again, on foot. I think I was glad about being on foot. Speed was dangerous and I didn't want to ride a bike ever again.

I woke up unable to move my body without pain. My eyes saw only the fabric with the white background and the ugly beige and pink flowers.

"I must have slept in a strain," I mumbled as I made my way out of bed. "It couldn't be the quilt."

That same night my life slides continued.

Cars were still going by the house slowly moving along allowing the passengers to stare wide-eyed through rolled up car windows. No one was going to stop and offer any assistance. The most the looky-loos would do was try to stifle the grins that were creeping up on the corners of each of their mouths.

I wanted to crawl into a hole and die. It was so embarrassing.

It surely was a sight to behold and hear too if you've a mind to listen to a squalling sixteen year old boy trying to stop what he considered as torture that was being applied to his body by the sheer guts and determination of his mother, my mother.

Lee was six foot tall weighing over two hundred pounds and he was trying to run from his mother of five foot four weighing in at about the same poundage.

"I promise I won't do it again. Please stop, mom! Please stop! I won't do it again, please!" he shouted as big crocodile tears rolled down his reddened face.

"Stand still, Lee. How can I give you a whipping that you deserve if you won't stand still?"

"Mom, you're killing me, please stop" he said as he ducked and dived out of the reach of the flicking leather belt.

"No, you won't do it again," snarled our angry mother as she swung the leather belt in the general direction of Lee's backside.

I watched the display that was occurring in our front yard with a growing embarrassment. I knew this episode would be the talk of the school the next day.

I turned my head away from the loud drama being played out in the front yard until I heard the sirens and caught a glimpse of the flashing lights. I ran out the door to see if my mother actually did kill my brother. I wouldn't have blamed her one single bit if she did.

"Mrs. Hudson, are you Mrs. Hudson?" asked the sheriff after he had climbed from his vehicle and stood with his arms on his hips in front of my already angry mother.

"Yes, what is it you want?" she sputtered. Her face was turning beet red and I wasn't sure if it was from embarrassment at having the sheriff standing in front of her or if it was the built up anger that Lee had caused.

"We received a call reporting the abuse of a child. Do you know anything about that?" he asked gruffly.

"I was whipping my son with a belt."

"Where is your son?"

"He went running around the house."

The sheriff took off walking as fast as he could so he could find the abused child.

I ran to the back door and sneaked out so I could see the sheriff's surprise when he saw the child that was being abused.

The sheriff obviously thought he was looking for a little boy because when he walked up to my blubbering brother he said, "Where is Mrs. Hudson's little boy?"

"That's me."

The sheriff's mouth fell open as he stared at Lee.

"How old are you?" demanded the confused sheriff.

"Sixteen," was Lee's sullen reply.

"Was your mother beating you?"

"She was whipping me with a belt, but it hardly touched me," he said with a smile that engulfed his round, freckled face.

"Then you aren't hurt?"

"No sir, not a bit. I'm faster than mom."

"Why were you crying, screaming, and carrying on like she was killing you?"

"I wanted her to stop."

The sheriff turned on his heel and walked toward the front of the house where he confronted my calmed down mother.

"Mrs. Hudson, your son says you hardly hurt him. Yet, he was screaming and carrying on like he was inches from death."

"He always does that."

"Why were you whipping him?"

"He cut school, again."

"Do you think that deserves a whipping with a belt?"

I was surprised my mother didn't tell him it was none

of his business, but she didn't say that at all. Maybe it was because he was the law.

"I've tried everything else. There's nothing left to do but issue a little pain for him to remember the next time he wants to cut school."

"Why does he skip school?"

"He doesn't want to go. The law says he has to go. What am I supposed to do?"

"Talk to his teachers, his guidance counselor, or someone that will offer you some advice."

"I can't."

"Why not?"

"I don't drive. Even if I did drive, I don't have a car."

"Call them."

"I don't have a telephone."

"Something has got to be done," said the exasperated sheriff.

"I was always made to believe that once my kids were in school, then it was up to the school to get them educated with no interference from the parents. If that's true, then they, I mean the school people, aren't doing their job. Isn't that right?"

"I guess so. What about Mr. Hudson?"

"What about him?"

"He could talk to someone."

"He works out of town and doesn't get home but about every two weeks on the weekend. When should he talk to them?"

"What's your son's name?"

"Lee."

"Why doesn't Lee want to go to school?"

"They make fun of him because he's slow."

"Well, I don't know what to tell you, Mrs. Hudson. I don't want to be called out here again for child abuse even though your child is bigger than you are."

"I'll talk to his father. The only thing we have left is to let him quit school and go to work at anything he can find."

"That might be for the best," offered the sheriff as he walked toward his vehicle.

I smiled when I heard her tell the sheriff that she was going to let Lee quit school. That's what he wanted to do and I wanted him to do that, too. He would no longer embarrass me as I walked through the long hallways at school. I would no longer have to live in his shadow of being a bully and not too bright, if you know what I mean.

Now, as I look back at that day I see a bittersweet memory, I'm sorry that my brother was allowed to quit school even though I knew the only way he was ever going to graduate would be based on his age.

There were no special education classes for my brother to help him learn what he needed to know to make his life better. He was and is a slow learner. His lack of education would keep him a common laborer for the rest of his life.

My brother is now over sixty years old. He lives in an old rundown, ram shackled house that belongs to his third wife who has passed on to a better place. He has had a stroke and is barely getting by.

Life has been rough for my brother.

CHAPTER 12

THE 4-H TRIP

Most of the time I wore homemade dresses made of fabric that was created for old women. Girls wearing pants was a new thing and shorts were out of the question.

Dad was stern and wrote all of the rules in my world. Occasionally I broke those rules.

Mr. Higgins, the 4-H leader that lived up the hollow, wanted to take us to an amusement park about a hundred miles from home. There were six of us that had formed the 4-H group. Mr. Higgins was an avid amateur photographer and was into teaching us all about taking pictures, good pictures, that year.

Dad was working in another state at the time and I didn't think he would be a problem. My only obstacle would be mom and, of course, money.

I had some money saved up from doing odd jobs for people. Dad believed everyone should work for his wages that is, of course, unless you were working at your own home. That was free work. No one got paid for that kind of work, not at our house. There was no allowance for us kids. We only got lunch money and money for special reasons from dad and mom.

I would iron for the lady who lived across the road on the hill. It was Carol's mother who paid me to do her ironing and scrubbing her kitchen floor on my hands and knees. It was hard work but she did pay me for it.

Mrs. Warnock paid me to do some yard work when Lee mowed her grass. That was hard work, too. I had to get down on my hands and knees and trim the grass next to all of the sidewalks. I was tired when I finished that job every week.

"Mom, Mr. Higgins is taking the 4-H members to the amusement park this weekend. Can I go?"

"Your dad will be home. You'll have to ask him."

"He won't let me go. I thought he wasn't coming home this weekend. He was just here last weekend."

"He lost his job."

"What happened?"

"They moved the company out of the country. He lost his job."

Dad came home Friday night and I didn't ask to go to the amusement park.

Saturday morning I got up early got myself cleaned up and dressed to go play in the only pair of shorts I owned and those were hand-me-downs.

"Mom, I'm going to go to Sally's house this morning.

I'll be there most of the day because her mom and dad are going shopping and Sally doesn't like to stay home alone."

"Okay, Ellen, but get home before dark," said my dad as mom nodded her head in agreement.

"If it gets too late, Sally's dad will drive me home because they want me to stay with Sally."

They didn't pay any attention to me after I walked out the front door. Dad went to the bathroom to shave and mom was in the kitchen making breakfast for them both.

When I got to the gate, I jumped into the ditch that ran alongside the road. It was dry because there had been no recent rain. I hunkered down as low as I could get to the ground without actually crawling and followed the ditch past the open field where dad had one of his two gardens. When the ditch came to an end I jumped up to road level and hunkered down behind the hedges that guarded the front of the Warnock's house. Once I got past the hedges, I knew mom and dad couldn't see me from the house.

I walked rapidly and glanced back over my shoulder every few moments hoping and praying that they wouldn't catch me. I was walking in the opposite direction of where I told them I was going.

I was going to the amusement park with the 4-H gang. Staying all day with Sally was a lie. Sally didn't have a telephone and dad didn't know where she lived so I knew he couldn't check up on me.

Mr. Higgins loaded us all into the back of his pick-up truck. When he made the turn that would take him directly passed the front of my house, I ducked down as low as I could so I couldn't be seen by mom and dad.

I was so excited about going to the amusement park but I was so scared that something horrible might happen and I would get into some really big trouble.

The day was fun as long as I didn't dwell on the fact that I had to sit while the others rode the carnival rides. I didn't have enough money to do everything they did but I had enough to keep me happy.

When we climbed back into the truck we were all sunburned, tired and hungry. The cool air in the open pick-up truck was going to feel good on the sunburns.

Mr. Higgins wanted to let me off at my house but I told him he had to drive past the house so I could get out and walk home from the opposite direction. It wasn't until I made that statement that he knew I had slipped off without permission. That was the last time he took us for an out of town trip.

By the time I walked into the house, dad had gone to bed, and mom was in the living room on the sofa sleeper where I also slept.

"Did you have a good time?" she asked me when I crawled into bed.

"Yeah, great," I said as I stifled a yawn.

She rose from bed wearing her rose printed, homemade nightgown and made her way to the bathroom.

Quilted Memories

The rose printed fabric floated in front of my eyes like a flag waving.

When I woke up the square of rose printed fabric was covering my eyes.

"Mom knew," I mumbled as I forced myself to get up.

The next night I endured the rebroadcast of my eighth grade graduation. The blue and white gingham checked fabric dress that I wore to the ceremony was cut and sewn into many places on the brightly colored quilt.

"Dad, can I buy a new store-bought dress to wear to my eighth grade graduation?" I asked hoping he would say yes.

"Don't you have a dress to wear?"

"Just the ones mom made. They aren't dressy and they don't look very good when all the other girls in my class are wearing new store-bought dresses."

"We'll see if we can find one this weekend."

"Thanks, Dad. I'll need dressy shoes, too."

I knew I was pushing my luck but I asked for the shoes anyway.

When we went dress shopping, dad dropped mom and me in front of the clothing store and he went elsewhere for a little while.

"What size do you need," asked the elderly sales clerk.

"I don't know. I've never bought a new dress."

136

She looked at me like I was telling her the biggest lie in the world. It was true though because I had always worn hand-me-downs and mom made dresses, I had no idea what size I wore.

The only dress in the entire store that we could find to fit my short fat body was the size 14 blue and white gingham checked dress with the white collar edged in lace. We found a pair of white dressy heels to go with the dress and I was all set for 8th grade graduation.

Dad didn't go to the ceremony. He wasn't much of a people person. He surely didn't like crowds of any type. He took us to the door and let us out saying that he would pick us up after the shindig.

Even though I had a pretty new dress and new shoes, my heart dropped when I saw what my classmates were wearing.

My dress emphasized that I was still quite young and not quite ready for the dresses of the adult world. My classmates were wearing outfits that models would have worn in magazine spreads.

Once again I was the odd one out. I was certainly glad that the dress that I was trying to hide would be covered by a black graduation gown.

After the ceremony a party was to be held in the gymnasium for the participants and their families. Mom and I couldn't stay because dad was picking us up directly after the ceremony. I wouldn't have wanted to stay at that time even if I had the chance. I was too embarrassed.

Quilted Memories

When I arrived at the house, I immediately took off the new dress and stuffed it in the back of the closet. I never wore it again. Mom gave it to my sister-in-law to be included in the quilt.

My new shoes were never worn again either. The heels were a bit spiky, they weren't high, but the heels narrowed to a tiny point. I had felt funny when I was wearing them but I didn't take them off to see what the problem was. On both shoes the narrow spiky part of the heel had folded over forcing me to walk at an odd angle. Those pretty new shoes went into the trash.

The blue and white gingham checked fabric danced in front of my eyes on the quilt when I woke up from a restless sleep.

CHAPTER 13

VISITING KARIN

I lived through the nightmare of my eighth grade graduation but my visit to Karin's house could have cost me my life. The old shorts and the ugly blouse my mom made me caused that memory. God, how I hated those homemade clothes.

Mom and dad had finally pulled from the driveway going to southern Ohio. I watched the white Ford Fairlane as it made its way along the city street until it faded from view.

"Yes," I said as I pumped my arm in emphasis. "Now I can go visit Karin."

It was going to be a long walk because Karin lived on West 44th Street and I lived on West 11th, but what the heck. Mom and dad were gone and I had a couple of hours to get there before it would even begin to get dark.

I looked up at the sky and noticed rapidly moving clouds. I should be able to get there before it rains, I reasoned, if it rains at all. Cleveland being located on the shores of Lake Erie sometimes had to endure rapidly changing lake-effect weather, but that usually happened in the winter time when mountains of snow would cascade down on the city hiding all of its blemishes under a pristine blanket of white fluff.

I walked and walked, glancing at the sky as it seemed to be changing colors from gray to a bright orange to yellow and back to gray. The clouds were stacking upon each other. The wind began to blow and I saw the heavily leaved limbs of the trees nearly touching the ground.

"It isn't supposed to rain," I mumbled as I held my eyes to the sky.

I'm not a gazelle so I wasn't surprised to find myself struggling to maintain my balance on the cracked sidewalk.

"I'm so clumsy, must have tripped on a crack," I said as I felt myself redden with embarrassment. I looked around me but I saw no one who might have seen me trip and almost fall on my face.

"That's odd," I said aloud without fear of being heard talking to myself. "There is absolutely no one out here. What is going on?" I asked myself as I turned my body a complete three hundred sixty degrees looking for people.

I continued to walk without any thought that I might be headed for trouble.

Up ahead I could see the sidewalks clearing of people who were running for cover into their houses. Cover from what? What's happening?

I must continue to walk. I'm only about half way to

Karin's house so deciding to turn around and head back home wasn't an option. Besides, the clouds were building up and changing colors in both directions. There was no escaping whatever temper tantrum Mother Nature was deciding to pull right now.

The thunder started. That rumble explained the light show that had been taking place behind the clouds.

I started counting, "1-1000, 2-1000, 3-1000, 4-1000, 5-1000 - that's supposed to tell me how many miles away the actual storm is."

I stopped walking so I could hear another rumble start up.

"1-1000, 2-1000, 3-1000, 4-1000 – it's almost here," I said as I looked around me for shelter. "Trees, don't stand under the trees, don't stand near the metal fence, where could I go to get shelter?"

Most of the houses in the area where I was walking were abandoned because the City of Cleveland in all of its power and glory were tearing down the neighborhoods that I had grown up in and building freeways. The structures standing on each side of the road were physically unsafe, but they were also dangerous in other ways. Anybody could be hidden inside them in the darkness waiting to spring out at some poor unsuspecting souls to rob or kill them where they stood. I didn't want to be one of those poor unsuspecting souls.

I continued to walk.

I saw the trees swaying back and forth furiously,

angrily, like they were trying to shake every leaf off of their mighty limbs. One tree was bent over so far that I thought it would break. Instead the mighty tree popped back up and continued to try to shake itself free of the wind.

"Snap, crack, boom!"

I spun myself around to see a huge tree I had walked past moments before fall across the street crushing everything in its path.

"Oh, God, where can I go?" I screamed as I started running.

Tree trash and debris started blowing about in front of me. I could hear wood cracking and breaking behind me. I was afraid to look back to see what was being destroyed. It really didn't sound like the tree I had heard previously. I knew it was a house being blown apart by that terrific force of the wind as it traveled along the same street I was traveling on.

I finally reached West 30th street. Fourteen more blocks, that's all I needed to go to get to the safety of Karin's house.

I hadn't asked dad and mom to drop me off at Karin's house as they left town, because I knew the answer would have been "no".

"You don't need to go bothering those people," was what my dad would have told me. "Stay home or we're going to make you go with us the next time."

I was thirteen years old. I didn't need a baby-sitter and

I surely didn't want to go on that long drive and be bored out of my mind for two days. There was no television or anything to do when we went there to check on the house that mom and dad planned to retire to someday.

Of course, my older brother Lee was supposed to keep an eye on me and see that I didn't get into trouble, but I knew that wasn't going to happen. He actually disappeared from the landscape to go hang out with friends before dad and mom pulled out of the driveway.

I didn't want to be alone. I was afraid of being alone. So – I was going to visit Karin.

I couldn't stand it anymore. I had to look behind me. The noise was getting louder and louder with the sounds of lumber crashing against the pavement or perhaps against other houses.

My eyes stared in terror at what I was seeing. I continued to walk in the direction opposite of where I was seeing the destruction with my head turned as far around on my shoulders as my neck would allow.

There was a roof from a house stationed in the middle of the street. The shingles were still intact. It looked as if the wind had slid its mighty fingers beneath the eaves, gently lifting it up, and carefully setting it down on its new location. I didn't see the structure from which it has been removed.

I saw doors and windows and gutters and anything and everything that could be pulled away from its moorings by the wind, strewn on the ground next to and in front of the roof. It looked as if pieces of glass were spinning around in the wind cutting into and slicing all objects in their path.

I snapped by head around to see that there wasn't any flying glass in front of me.

I tried to run faster. I had to get away from this destruction that might lead to my death.

How was I going to explain that I was sliced to ribbons on West 31st Street when I was supposed to be on West 11th Street?

What a stupid question, I would be dead. I wouldn't have to explain anything. Mom and dad would feel really sorry that they had ever trusted me.

Would they get into trouble for leaving me at home while they went out of town?

"The sound, what was that? It sounds like a freight train. I'm not walking close to any railroad tracks. What is that?"

I looked up and I saw what appeared to be a huge spinning top dipping its tail down to the ground.

"A tornado!" I cried as I tried to run faster to get away from the tail that was dancing around just behind me.

The rain that had only been wind driven splashes suddenly came down with such a force that I covered my head with my arms to keep that damage down to a minimum. I needed to look up to find a street sign but I was afraid the rain would put out my eyes.

My run was just a walk as I forced myself forward

against the wind that was now in front of me. I could feel small pieces of debris flying against me banging me everywhere.

Then it stopped, it was quiet. No wind was blowing, actually the sun was trying to shine.

I pulled my arms down to my sides and stood still with my mouth hanging open.

There was absolutely no movement going on around me.

I glanced at the street sign, West 44th Street, was displayed in bright white letters against a Christmas green background.

The silence was eerie. I knew I had to get to Karin's house fast, really fast.

"Not much further," I said as I tried to encourage myself to press on to the safety and warmth of Karin's family and house.

I saw a tree that had fallen across West 44th Street exposing its gigantic roots to the air. I made my way around the tree and walked on to the beckoning safety.

"There it is!" I shouted as I started running again.

I reached the front porch and started banging on the front door.

"Ellen, where did you come from?" asked Karin's mom as she opened the door wide enough for me to enter into the living room.

"I walked. I didn't know there was a tornado coming. Can I stay here for a while?" I said as I sobbed in her arms.

"Sure, sure, come on in. Karin's not here. She went to stay with her brother. You should have called, you know."

"I don't have a telephone."

"I'll get you a towel. You can sit here and dry off for a while. After all of the wind settles down, I'll have the mister drive you home."

"Thanks," I said softly.

I wasn't really that disappointed when I didn't find Karin at home. It wasn't specifically her company I was seeking. I was seeking the comfort and safety of her home that was filled with the warmth of a family.

I didn't want to be alone. I was afraid to be alone.

CHAPTER 14

REALLY LUCKY

The royal blue block of fabric reminded me of my high school graduation robe that brought forth some good memories of some teachers I was proud to know.

I've been lucky, really lucky, because I have had the good fortune of being taught by some super fine people during my school years. I've also had some losers, but we won't discuss them, not now anyway.

When I started school, we had no kindergarten. I know this dates me a bit, but that's life as I have lived it and shared it with others.

First grade was traumatic.

My older brother had been brow beaten by an angry first grade teacher by the name of Mrs. Miller. He hated school and I knew if I drew Mrs. Miller as my first grade teacher, I would hate school, too.

We were herded into one classroom that certainly wasn't big

enough to hold all of us. Mrs. Miller was the larger than life adult standing in front of us and my heart sank slowly into my chest. She looked mean. Her voice had no friendliness in it. It was harsh and screechy loud.

"Sit down," she shouted at the crowd. "Everyone who can find a seat, please sit. All others line up against that blackboard."

Many of the students around me were crying. I wasn't crying but it wouldn't have taken much to get me started.

As we stood cowering from Mrs. Miller's loud tones, a short, round lady by the name of Mrs. Gregory entered the room. She had a list of names that she started reading.

"Scot Anderson, Ginger Reedy, Michael Thompson, April Owens, Ellen Hudson, and on and on."

I was one of those names. I was Ellen Hudson. She had instructed us to stand in the hallway and wait for her to finish reading the list.

We had no idea what was happening. When we were told that we were being added to her classroom I breathed a sigh of relief. I was so grateful to be away from the evil Mrs. Miller.

Mrs. Gregory was a nice lady and I was lucky enough to have her as a teacher for first and second grade.

She ruled her classroom but she had a velvet touch. I remember earning my one and only paddling during my school years from her. I had been snooping in the trash can looking for the list of grades she had thrown out. I wanted to see what I was going to be getting on my report card.

She caught me and out came that little wooden paddle.

"I won't ever do it again," I promised as my face turned

crimson from embarrassment.

Mrs. Ruby was my seventh grade English teacher. She was soft spoken with a warm sweet face that invited you to participate in learning.

She won me over in no time and I grew to trust her.

That was when I discovered that I truly wanted to write.

I had been taught all through the six previous grades that books were to be treasured. We were not permitted to mark in or dog ear any of the pages of our books. We were told to handle them with care at all times because of the expense of replacing the books.

"Your parents will have to pay for the books if you lose them or tear them in any way."

My daddy didn't have a job much of the time I was in elementary school due to being laid off from the railroad. He would have been upset with me if he had to buy a new book because of my carelessness.

I covered all of my textbooks with brown paper bags that I taped together as dust covers. I turned the pages slowly and carefully so as not to tear them in any way. I certainly didn't write in any of them. Others did, and I had books in my possession in which answers had been penciled on the pages all the way through the book. I erased all of the markings whenever I could.

The awe and reverence I held toward the books manifested itself into a deep desire to write books. I wanted to be the person whose name was written on the spine.

"I wrote that. Let me sign it for you," was what I dreamed of saying.

Quilted Memories

I had written many short stories and I wanted Mrs. Ruby to read the most recent one I had penciled. It wasn't good enough yet to write it in ink. I wanted to see what she thought of my need to write.

"Mrs. Ruby, would you read my story?"

"I'd love to, Ellen. I'll read it this weekend," she answered with her sweet smile.

I wanted her to stop whatever she was doing and read it then. I didn't want to have to wait and entire weekend, but I did. I sweated and worried over what she would think of me.

"Ellen, your story was very good. I liked it a lot but you need to do one thing before you make writing your life."

"What's that, Mrs. Ruby?" I asked as my heart sank in my chest.

"You need to live a little more. Grow up a little more. Learn everything you can learn about life so your words will ring true. You are writing about emotions that I'm sure you don't understand so give it a little time. Keep a good journal or record of your life and feelings. Then write."

She was right. I was writing about subjects I knew nothing about personally. I had only read about them in books.

I went home where I put my stories away in a box until such time as I felt I had lived enough and learned enough so that I would know what I was talking or writing about and my words would ring true.

My high school years introduced me to Mr. Brannan, my World History teacher, Mrs. Lester, my Algebra teacher, and Mrs. McDonough, my English teacher.

Mrs. Lester tried to teach me Algebra. She knew I tried but she also knew that it wouldn't stay in my head. Algebraic concepts were just beyond my comprehension because I had developed a mental block. In my mind I didn't think I could do the work, thus I wasn't able to understand Algebra.

I always attempted my homework. I struggled over it for hours and hours and I had plenty of paper to show the struggle.

I took every test and if it weren't for grading on the curve, I would not have passed any of them.

I believe I was the only student ever in her Algebra that can lay the claim to receiving a D1. The D represented the fact that she had allowed me to pass the course. The 1 represented the notion that she thought I had tried with all of my heart and soul and the highest number you could achieve in attitude.

Mrs. Lester would play an important role later in my school life.

Mr. Brannan was too handsome to be a school teacher especially around high school teenage girls. We all dreamed of him in our lives but definitely not in the role of teacher.

As an initiation prank to join the Future Teachers of America, a high school career club, the new members of the club had to propose to a teacher. You had to know that Mr. Brannan would be the one to get the most proposals. Mine was one of them.

"Mr. Brannan, will you marry me?" I shouted as I walked out of his classroom.

"Sure, when?"

I stopped in my tracks. I had not expected that answer.

"What?"

"Sure, I'll marry you? What day did you have in mind?" he said with a smile.

"The day after you divorce your wife," I responded with a matching smile.

I passed my initiation with flying colors and became an active member of the Future Teachers of America.

Mrs. McDonough was my twelfth grade English teacher. She encouraged me to read constantly, write daily, and to not give up on anything I wanted to do with my life. I helped her grade papers and keep up with her many daily chores.

The only bad grade I had received during my high school years was from Mrs. Lester and I can't say that I didn't deserve that bad grade.

Being a member of the National Honor Society had not been a goal or even an interest of mine until the day of the nominations. Then it became important. It was an honor to be that highly regarded and I wanted to be one of those people.

When nominations were being made for the National Honor Society, I thought my D1 in Algebra was going to be my downfall. My two girlfriends, Karin and Annie, were also being considered for the Honor Society and I thought they were shoe-ins. The National Honor Society had always been a goal of Karin's because her brother had been a member. Annie wanted to be a member because Karin wanted to be one.

I cringed when I discovered that Mrs. Lester was on the Honor Society Committee. Mrs. McDonough was also on the committee but Mrs. Lester was the Chairman. It was all over but for the crying, I thought.

The day of the announcement was a wonderful surprise for

me.

I made it. I was accepted into the National Honor Society.

Karin and Annie were not.

The National Honor Society became a wedge that caused the shattering of the friendships that I had with Annie and Karin. Things were never the same after they discovered that I had made it and they didn't.

My teachers made me who I am today. They told me I had to live, to learn, and to write. Thanks to their encouragement, that's what I'm doing.

CHAPTER 15

SIZE 12

I was wearing a Size 14 at the age of thirteen. It was that blue and white gingham dress I will never, ever forget. It took me a few years but I got down to a Size 12. The quilt pieces that were made of black polyester reminded me of that Size 12 and the black pants with the strings ties woven up the sides.

I remembered that particular size because I actually wore an article or two of clothing with Size 12 emblazoned on the label. Of course, you may not understand why I'm dreaming of a Size 12, but hang in there and I'll clue you in.

In my mind, Size 12 is average. Every super woman (any woman larger than Size 12) ought to be able to say that once in her lifetime she wore that mediocre number. But, alas, many people are smaller than a 12 and, believe it or not, there are lots of ladies who fit into that below normal or "little" category.

When I pass one of the "little" ladies on the street, I want to either shoot her or get down on my chubby knees and beg her to tell me her secret to entering and living in the world of the thin.

The "little" ladies do not meet my expectations of ever being a Size 12 and living to brag about it, because to those below normal people, a Size 12 is no brag – just fact. They would have to gain weight to accomplish the feat of wearing a Size 12. They wouldn't have to lose weight, which is the curse of those like me who are above normal or as I now prefer to say "super".

If the truth were known, I used to envy the "little" people and dream of being below normal myself. I discovered to my amazement and utter disappointment that the only way I could be below normal was in my dreams. Or – perhaps I could become a normal Size 12 if I contracted a terminal disease that abolished my appetite. Or – perhaps a Size 12 was possible if I entered the horrible world of the eating disorders such as anorexia and bulimia. I don't like those choices at all.

When I graduated from the eighth grade, I wore a Size 14. Even in my early days I don't remember ever being a Size 12.

I do remember the verbal and mental abuse I had to withstand issued by my peers. My clothes always looked like they should have adorned the bodies of old ladies, not a teenager.

I had no dates in high school and didn't go to my senior prom.

It wasn't until I was in college at night and working in

the daylight hours, after I reached a Size 12 that I was asked for a date.

So- fighting fat, loneliness, and the isolation caused by being overweight and not fitting into the mold of the normal woman have made me into the person I am today.

Now – to me – life beneath a Size 12 is only a fading vision and not a clear-cut reality.

When I forced myself to face facts, I uncovered the wonderful world of the above normal where I have lived most of my life.

Size 12 is my new vision or dream because I know it's possible. I've done it once, many, many years ago.

The super world, which is any size above a Size 12, is improving because the clothing manufacturers of the universe have finally realized that there is a market – a large market. Please pardon the pun.

As my size fluctuates up and down the size scale, all above a Size 12, I must have clothing to fit in each and every size as I fight the battle of controlling the bulges. Eliminating the bulges was something I discovered I was not able to do at a very early age.

I have learned to live with my additional weight out of self-preservation. As many people, many times, and for many different reasons have said, "you must learn to like yourself". If I don't like me, how can anyone else like me?

I tried to think thin. That didn't work.

I went on a starvation diet that let me see a Size 12 once. At that same Size 12, I became very sick as a result of that starvation diet. I had to start eating again to survive, but not at a Size 12.

I also became a cynic because I realized that the same people I had been around every day when I was larger than a Size 12 suddenly noticed me only because I was thinner.

I was still the same person. My eyes were open and I saw each of them but they were all blind to my being alive.

I tried diet pills when they were very strong and prescribed. I was wired for days when I took one. I didn't eat which was great. I, also, didn't sleep. I couldn't control my nerves. I didn't act like me.

While I didn't like what those pills were doing to me, my so-called friends were trying their very best to get any of my unused pills away from me for their own unprescribed reasons.

Needless to say, those didn't work because I refused to continue the prescription. Not because my health was in danger, but because my friend, Jack, was taking too many of my pills and that was not good because of his high blood pressure.

I tried the over the counter diet pills. I guess it was my mindset that was the problem. I knew they were mild – too mild. They didn't contain the necessary drug to make my brain think my stomach was full all the time. Needless to say, they didn't work.

I've tried the fat burners. They didn't work.

I've done the exercise bit on a stationary bike, the terrible treadmill, and walking. I hate the treadmill but I try to walk outdoors as often as possible with a promise to myself that I will go back to riding my bike every morning.

I've discovered all the physical activities above tone my body tightening all the flab so it doesn't wobble and wiggle as much, but they don't noticeably cause me any weight loss.

Don't get me wrong, I know I have to maintain an exercise program for my health and I try to do that whenever possible.

Hey, did you know you could gain weight on a fat free diet? I did!

I cut the fat in my diet without paying attention to the calories. That didn't work.

I believe my size is dictated in large part by my genes. Whether I like it or not, it will always be a battle for me.

Well, my only choice is to accept me as I am because I've tried my whole life to be something I'm not.

I will keep my dream of being a Size 12; it keeps me going and gives me a goal. I'm not going to cry about it if I don't get there. I've cried enough already.

I shall lift up my glass of Diet Coke in a toast to Size 12. I hope to see it again someday.

If not, oh well.

CHAPTER 16

SEARCHING FOR MR. RIGHT

While I was close to my Size 12, clothes became important and bright colors filled my closet with the quilt.

I was educated, that is to say that I had completed high school and worked my way through attaining three separate associate degrees at the local community college. Book learning was easy for me, but street learning was a much harder subject to tackle. Never the less, I was willing to tackle the obstacles and work my way through mazes and labyrinths in my search for the perfect "Mr. Right".

"Annie, are we going out tonight?"

"I don't know, Ellen. I may have to do an errand for my mother."

"Well, let me know before it gets too late. If we don't go out to where the men are, we won't meet "Mr. Right". We're getting to the age where finding that special someone is appearing to be more and more difficult."

"It seems that way, doesn't it?"

"Do you consider twenty-two to be old?"

"No, I certainly don't. Why would you ask me that question?" said an almost angry Annie.

"Well, think about it. How many unattached males in our age range have you met?"

"Come to think of it, not many. Maybe you're right."

"That's what I'm afraid of. Call me later and let me know about tonight."

Annie and I had led sheltered lives until we reached the age of twenty-one and decided to explore the world a little more.

We tired of the single bar scene and chose to attend college as night students. We would further our education, but we would also be able to meet men.

Annie's love labyrinth led her to a dead end relationship with Randy.

"Annie, where were you last week? I tried to call you all weekend."

"I flew to New York to see Randy."

"I thought he lived in New Jersey."

"He does. That's why we both flew to New York," explained a sad sounding Annie.

"He's married, isn't he?"

"Yes, but I didn't know until this past weekend," sobbed Annie into the napkin she had been holding on her lap.

"Why did he wait so long to tell you?"

"He said he was afraid I wouldn't see him anymore."

"Would you?"

"He waited too long and it's too late."

"Why is it too late?"

"Because I love him and I'm pregnant."

Annie eliminated the problem at a clinic on the east side of the city.

I met Joe, a guy who worked in the warehouse, at Tonodane.

"Ellen, you're looking great. Want to go to a concert with me this weekend?" he whispered as he stood in front of my desk.

I looked up at him and tearfully said, "Yes, I'd love to go with you."

For Joe, I would have been willing to do anything he asked me to do. I had lost fifty pounds on a near starvation diet to get the invitation. Now that I had been asked, I was floating in the air on a giant cloud of happiness.

The first and only date with Joe was ended with a kiss and "I'll see you at work on Monday."

I waited for days for a second date. When it wasn't forthcoming, I decided I needed to know why?

"Joe, did I do anything that you didn't like when we went to the concert?"

"No, I had a great time."

"Then why didn't we do it again?" I asked teary eyed.

"I was afraid to ask you again, Ellen. I didn't want it to lead to something serious. I have other plans for my life and, at the moment, it doesn't include a serious relationship. I want to be famous by joining or starting a rock band. I don't want to teach guitar to students who don't want to learn for the rest of my life. I want my life to matter."

"Oh, so do I. I want my life to matter to," I said in agreement.

"I could fall for you really hard, Ellen. Instead, I want to be friends. Is that all right with you?"

"Sure, Joe. No problem. We can be friends."

I cried myself to sleep for many nights.

Annie met Douglas, a black salesman who swept Annie off her feet from the moment she met him. The irony in that relationship was that Annie was a blonde-haired, green-eyed Polish girl who was from a family of racists. They weren't Klan members but the only thing missing was the membership card.

Annie met Douglas in out of the way places where the mixing of races was accepted. Those kinds of places were hard to find in the 70's.

Once again, Annie fell head over heels for a married man. Once again, she was not told the truth until it was too late. Once again, Annie was pregnant.

Annie's life maze took her to the clinic where she made her problem go away and caused major damage to her mental state.

I met and married Ed who had impregnated me and then lowered his lofty life plan threshold enough to marry me.

My labyrinth led to abuse, pain, and a second child before I was able to find my path back to force myself to take another turn.

As soon as I made the turn to divorce, I discovered I was pregnant again. A third child was totally unwanted and unacceptable. I visited the same clinic that Annie had visited.

Annie survived the second trip to the clinic but her mind wouldn't accept the guilt. She drove herself to thinking that she needed tranquilizers to calm her down, sleeping pills to put her to sleep at night with the mind games of guilt that she endured every night, and something that would wake her up every morning so she could go to work and start all over.

Annie and I had drifted apart. I made the first step to pull us closer together. I was sure my marriage to Ed had caused the split. I no longer needed my bar hopping girlfriend to spend after work hours with.

"Ted, where's Annie?"

"In the hospital."

"What happened? Is she all right?"

"Did you know she was taking any drugs?"

"What? What drugs?" I sputtered in the telephone.

"The doctor said she has had some kind to drug interaction. It appears that she was going to several different doctors and not letting each of the doctors know what the other was prescribing. She is now in a coma in a fetal position. They don't think she'll ever come out of the coma. Annie is going to die, Ellen," sobbed a heartbroken older brother.

I toiled eight years without marrying a second time. During

those eight years I met Jack, a married man. He told me he was married but that he was in the process of getting a divorce.

I believed him.

"Jack, can you go to the company dance with me?"

"No, I can't."

"I didn't even tell you the date. How can you already say no?"

"You know my situation, Ellen. I can't let anyone catch me with another woman until the divorce it final."

"When will that be?"

"I don't know."

"Has it even been filed?"

"Let's change the subject, Ellen."

"You're not getting a divorce, are you? All these months, you've made love to me and then went home to your wife. You didn't have to take care of your kids because she was still there. Am I right?"

Jack didn't answer me. He didn't have to.

I discovered I was pregnant again but this time I truly wanted the child because I loved Jack with all of my heart and soul.

"Jack, I'm pregnant," I said as I smiled broadly.

"Get rid of it," shouted Jack as his eyes glistened with anger.

"Why?"

"I don't want another kid. I will not support another kid. That's why my wife and I were separated for those months because she, too, was pregnant. I told her to get an abortion or I wouldn't take her back. She did and that's why I'm at home."

"You don't ever intend to marry me, do you, Jack?"

"Not at this time."

"When?"

"I don't know but get rid of the kid or it will never, ever happen," he snarled as he stormed out of my apartment.

Jack paid half of the cost and I made a second trip to the clinic.

I left the city and Jack behind when I moved two hundred fifty miles south.

Annie remained in a coma.

I met and married Mike after a whirlwind courtship. Mike was the father of two daughters who were approximately the same ages of my two sons. The marriage lasted six months mainly because the kids fought every time they were in the same room together. I decided life was too short to have to spend all of my time as a referee.

Annie woke up and had to learn how to live all over again. The only contact she had with me was a Christmas card each year.

I met Sonny and married the man to whom I plan to remain married to until my dying days.

Annie never met anyone to marry but she took on the job of trying to convert the world to her religion.

Annie and I exchange Christmas cards every year.

This year my Christmas card came back – undeliverable.

CHAPTER 17

TAN PAISLEY PRINT

I yanked the quilt off the bed, folded it, and placed it in the closet. The weather was getting too warm for the heavy heat produced by the quilt. My mind was becoming numb from the abuse it forced into my dreams at night. I needed a break from the memories.

All the rest of the summer I was not bothered by instant replays of my life. My mind was rested and refreshed. I decided it was time to add the quilt to my bed when the first hint of frost hit the outdoor air.

The paisley printed tan fabric wallpapered my mind.

I was pregnant and I didn't want anyone to know about it. I had to make some clothes that were larger in size and would allow me to expand in the belly without a lot of people noticing the additional weight gain.

The peasant style was popular at the time so that seemed to help when I looked for an adaptable pattern. The dress pattern I chose was hemmed and gathered at the neckline and sleeve edges. The pattern also indicated a blousy gathering at the waistline but I didn't use that particular instruction. Instead, I allowed the dress to flow loose and free giving me plenty of room to grow and expand.

I was living at home and unmarried. I had to do something and do it quickly.

"I'm pregnant," I told Jude one hot July night while I was sitting in his mother's car. Jude didn't have a car of his own. He was still living at home with his parents and attending college.

"Are you sure?" he asked angrily.

"I have morning sickness. I throw up every single morning when I get to work. I have no doubt that I'm pregnant."

"When do you want to get married?"

"I don't unless you really want to do that. I don't want to force you into doing anything. I'll have this baby by myself if I have to," I said as I tried to hold back the tears that had been making their presence known for days.

"I'm the father. I should marry you. I will marry you. I love you, Ellen."

Every time I had to share my secret with someone else, I was wearing that tan paisley print dress.

"Mom, Ellen and I are getting married," said Jude as he faced his mother's wrath.

"Why?" she snapped.

"We love each other," he said timidly.

"You've got to finish college, get a job, get a place to live, before you even think about getting married, Jude. You should know better unless there is another reason for this sudden announcement."

"I love..." sputtered Jude.

"I'm pregnant," I said as I jumped into the conversation.

"With whose baby?" she demanded.

"Jude's," was my only answer.

"You've been sleeping around, Ellen. I've been told that you have been sleeping with a bunch of men," she spit the words at me like they were poison.

"Jude, are you going to help me?"

"Mom, Ellen and I are going to get married."

"Tell her, Jude. Tell her that I was a virgin when we made love. Tell her, please," I cried as I ran from the room.

Jude could only nod his head in agreement.

I was wearing the tan paisley printed dress again.

"Dad, Jude and I are getting married," I blurted out one evening while we were all sitting at the dinner table.

Dad looked at me and smiled. He knew the reason for the sudden announcement of marriage. I didn't have to tell him anything.

I remembered the letter I had written to him many years later. It was a letter that he didn't get to read, not in this world anyway.

Dearest Dad,

You didn't stand very tall at only five feet seven inches and your gray hair made you fade into the background. You would watch us with your soft, brown eyes that were always lit with love.

When we, my brother and I, were young you would let us go as far as you felt it was safe, but you jerked hard on the heart strings when we were leaning towards trouble.

As adults you waited for us to ask for your guidance. You didn't interfere in our separate lives, but it wasn't for lack of interest or love. On the contrary, you let us go our separate ways because you loved and trusted us.

The only time I can recall you showing me that you could be physical was when I was so very young. That was all it took - one time.

Many people have told me that I can't possibly remember something that happened when I was two years old, but I do. I remember it as vividly as if it happened yesterday.

We moved from Virginia to Ohio following the path that railroad employment had led you. We were living in a small house with outdoor bathroom facilities and no fenced yard.

"Ellen, I don't want you slipping off and bothering the neighbors. You stay in the back yard," you said sternly.

I smiled at you and you smiled in return and went back to working. You were always working either at the railroad yards or at home in the garden that you planted each year to feed us. You had a lot to do to keep us all fed and clothed.

The neighbor's yard was luring me to cross the mind fence you had erected.

I crossed that mind fence and you spotted me.

"Ellen, get in the house now!" you bellowed.

I took off running. I arrived at the back door at about the same time you did. I stood on my tiptoes trying to get the screen door open.

You opened the door for me with one hand while in the other hand you held a piece of kindling wood. You held it up high over me, the wood I mean, and told me to go sit on the gray couch in the living room.

"See this," you said as you menacingly shook the piece of kindling wood. "I'm going to use it on your bottom if you slip off again."

I sat on that old gray couch that I hate to this day and didn't move for what seemed to be hours.

When you spoke, I listened really hard.

Finally you had to walk past me as you went to find something in your bedroom.

"Daddy?" I asked softly so I wouldn't incur your wrath again.

"What, Ellen?"

"Can I get off the couch?"

"I never told you to stay on that couch. I told you not to go next door. Now go play."

I ran outside. I was released from a prison of my own making.

In a heartbeat you were gone.

As an adult I have tried to be good – the type of good that I know you would want me to be.

It wasn't until I was an adult that I realized that mean, strict, selfish man was watching out for me and my brother.

170

It wasn't until I was a mother, a divorced one at that, that I discovered that you really did love me. If you hadn't loved me, you wouldn't have cared how I would have to face my future. You wouldn't have cared about what my life would be like when you weren't around to lead me through it. You could have just washed your hands of the whole sorry mess I call my life.

You knew I made some mistakes, some bad mistakes, but you waited for me to ask you for your help. You wouldn't jump into my life and tell me what to do. I wouldn't have listened to you if you did that to me.

You loved my sons like they were your own.

You knew my marriage wouldn't last even though you gave me verbal credit for having endured it for five years. You told me you guessed it wouldn't last much past one year. Thanks for the vote of confidence, Dad. You knew I really tried.

You've been gone for more than twenty years and yet a day does not pass that I don't wish that you were here with me to teach me, lead me, and guide me onto the right path to life and everyday living.

I miss those soft, brown eyes that were always lit up with love even when you were angry with me.

Every once in a while I look up and I know you're watching me. That's when I smile.

Thanks, Dad, for being there. I don't think I could have made it without you.

Words will never be able to tell you what's in my heart. I know that where you are you can see the love that will never die.

Please accept this letter from my heart.

Always your daughter,

Ellen

The leftover tan paisley print fabric was left with my mother and she added it to the bag of fabric that went to my sister-in-law.

When I awoke from my nightmares of pregnancy, I felt my stomach turn over as soon as I saw the tan paisley print fabric that was highlighted on the quilt by a lamp angled toward the bed directing its beam directly at the colorful square of cloth. I jumped out of bed and barely made it to the bathroom before vomiting. Even the thoughts of morning sickness made me throw up.

It was hard for me to think about my dad for any reason without getting all teary eyed and sad. Dad was a hard disciplinarian and stern man but I loved him with all of my heart because I knew he loved me and was only trying to help.

The quilt had no remnants of clothing for my dad sewn into its seams. Never the less, one piece of fabric that had a white background and tiny blue designs bordered by light blue pin stripes looked exactly like the material of the shirt dad was wearing the last time I saw him.

It couldn't have been the same fabric. In my heart I knew it was just something similar but my mind focused in on the memory in my dreams.

CHAPTER 18

THE WHITE PICKET FENCE

Once again, the white block with the blue designs and stripes surfaced in my dreams.

"Ellen?" my mother whispered weakly into the telephone.

In order for her to call me, there had to be a dire emergency. She disliked using a telephone for any reason.

"What, Mom?" I questioned as I paused for a moment trying to focus my thoughts on her fading voice. "Is anything wrong?" I asked loudly trying to force her to speak louder.

"Your dad says he can't breathe," she blurted out before she started crying.

"I'll be right there," I said as I slammed down my receiver while reaching for my blue jeans and tee shirt.

I quickly slipped my feet into my old tennis shoes and raced into the living room to locate my handbag.

"Sonny," I shouted. "Dad's sick. I've got to leave. Make sure Eddy and Aaron get ready for school. I'll be back as soon as I can," I added as I ran out the front door.

Sonny, Eddy, Aaron, and I lived in a well-worn, rented house less than two miles from my mom and dad's home. Two miles doesn't seem very far away until you hear that your dad can't breathe; then, it seems like a million miles.

"God, I hope she has the gate open," I prayed loudly as I pushed the gas pedal to the floor accelerating my speed many miles per hour over the speed limit that was forty-five on that stretch of Route 139.

"Dad and his white picket fence?" I muttered as I got closer to the house. "If I had a nickel for every hour's worth of work he wasted on the upkeep of that white picket fence, I would never have to worry about paying my bills on time ever again."

I remembered watching him when I was a little girl as he painstakingly measured each picket, cut it to the exact length and angle needed before he nailed it to the two by fours that were used to secure the pickets.

We were not allowed to climb the fence at any time because the pressure of our weight would break off some of the pickets that had been weakened by age. Needless to say, Lee and I never admitted to breaking any of the pickets even though it was usually our carelessness that caused the fence to take on the appearance of a smile with a missing tooth. Of course, we blamed each other for the destructive deed never once letting my dad know which one of us had done the actual misdeed. So, dad had to punish both of us or just forget about it and repair the fence, which is what he usually did.

Thankfully the gate was open and it was anchored against the fence with a loop of wire allowing me to pull directly into the driveway. I didn't have to stop the car while pressing the horn, holding up traffic, until mom slowly hauled her three hundred pounds out the front door, down the steps, across the yard to the fence where she would have to remove the wire hooked over the fence post and a picket. Next, she would have to back up her awkward body towards the fence on the side of the lot, stand and wait while I pulled into the driveway, then close the gate.

What a pain that can be when there is a lot of traffic, not to mention the fact that it is dangerous because so many people pulled out of the traffic line and drove around your waiting car without any kind of warning. Dad's car had been rear-ended more than once as he tried to negotiate the left turn into the safety of the graveled driveway.

I pulled the car towards the back of the house, slammed the gear into park, and jumped out almost before it stopped moving.

When I saw dad, I understood the telephone call. He was gasping for every breath. He had managed to walk to his recliner chair but I knew he could go no further.

"Dad," I said in an even but firm tone, "I'm calling an ambulance. You need some help, now."

Living in a rural area can be a problem when you are

trying to get an ambulance dispatched. But, low and behold, the very object I had silently cursed many times, was the landmark that would be used to locate the house.

"It's the house in Twin Valley on Route 139 with the white picket fence around it."

"Old man Hudson's place? It's the only one around with a white picket fence. Makes it real easy to find," said the dispatcher as he wrote down the directions.

"Yes, that's it. Please hurry. He can hardly breathe."

"Yes ma'am."

Now we had to wait. Seconds ticked slowly by, stretching into minutes, too many minutes.

I watched him gasp and struggle to try to drag into his cancerous lungs just a little bit of oxygen. He would close his eyes and reopen them as wide as possible as he tried to suck in all the air around him.

His eyes looked to me for help, but I couldn't give him any. I wanted so much to let him have some of my air. I had more than enough. I would gladly share what I had with my dad.

"What's taking them so long to get here?" I whispered loudly to my mother who was sitting on the sofa watching dad grow weaker and weaker with each loud intake of air; air that was not getting to his lungs.

Of course, I knew why it was taking so long for the ambulance to arrive. First the dispatcher had to contact the emergency personnel, medics for short, either by a loud horn that was sounded in the Rubyville community which was about five miles away, or by two-way radio, or by telephone. After the initial notice was given and contact made, the medics had to drive from their respective homes to the Rescue Squad Building where the ambulance was garaged. After getting the location and directions to the house of the person needing the help, the medics climbed into the ambulance and started driving. It all took time – too much time.

What could you expect with an all-volunteer service? I guessed this way was better than nothing, wasn't it?

More than thirty minutes after I placed the call for help, I heard the sirens.

Dad's vital signs were taken and he was strapped down to a cot, carried to the ambulance, and finally given oxygen.

With sirens wailing, red lights flashing, they drove off into the opposite direction from whence they had come. They were taking dad to Mercy Hospital that was over ten miles away.

I liked living in a rural community most of the time. I longed for a large, bustling, vibrant city when events like medical emergencies arose. I knew help would arrive quickly in a city.

While waiting for the ambulance I had called Sonny and told him to tell the boys not to worry and that I was taking their grandmother to the hospital to be with their grandfather. Mom couldn't drive so I knew I was in for the long haul.

Dad's doctor was at the hospital making his rounds

when dad was taken to the emergency room. When the doctor was notified of dad's arrival, he admitted dad to the hospital right away and dad was taken to a room where he was given oxygen at its highest level.

I made sure mom had a seat next to dad's bed then I went in search of an answer.

Three weeks earlier, dad's doctor had told us that dad had about six months to live, but only three weeks had passed since that declaration.

"What's happening with my dad?" I asked the doctor who was standing at the nurse's station looking at a medical chart.

The doctor looked up at me, recognizing me immediately because I had been with dad at the hospital three weeks earlier when the medical tests were being performed.

"Everything is being done to keep him comfortable without too much suffering, but he won't be going home again," he said as he respectfully lowered his eyes. "He waited too long to do anything about the pain he had been suffering."

"I know," I replied as I fought back the wave of tears building behind my eyes.

"We all knew he was sicker than he let on but he wouldn't do anything about it. I'm sure he knew he had cancer; he just didn't want to be told in so many words."

I remembered dad telling my mom that cancer would kill him someday. It was the very same disease that had killed his mother whose funeral was what had brought on the startling revelation.

I was only six years old at the time but I listened to what they were talking about and I remembered.

I also knew in my heart that the very same fate was lying in wait to enter my future.

Most everyone in my family had succumbed to the ravages of cancer so my hopes of dying peacefully in my sleep were nonexistent.

I walked away from the nurse's station toward the sterile hospital room where I would have to sit with mom and watch him fight for each remaining breath.

I didn't tell mom what the doctor told me, I didn't have to.

Dad couldn't talk; it took too much energy and oxygen to spit out the words.

I watched his gone-soft muscular body consisting of five feet seven inch height that was shorter than the average male stretched onto average sized bones. His weight usually stayed about the same, neither too heavy nor too light – just average.

This average man had a heart that was big enough to withstand the punishment and worry brought on by all of our problems. He absorbed those problems, large and small, like a sponge and went about his business of helping my brother or me get out of the predicament that had cornered us, forcing us to cry out for his help.

He was the smartest man I had ever met, but when I

was a child I didn't know that. It never occurred to me that you could be smart without the book learning that had been thrown at us daily in the schools.

Dad was what I called living-smart.

He knew how to fix things from broken furniture to broken hearts.

We, my brother and myself, knew he would be there for us any time we asked. He didn't force his opinion on to us; we had to ask.

How were we going to get by without having that average man to lean on?

The struggle for air seemed to let up for an hour or two as the life-sustaining oxygen passing through the clear plastic tube into the plastic mask covering his nose and mouth forced its way into his lungs.

The nurses were in and out checking this, monitoring that, but to say that they were actually helping him – they weren't. There was nothing they could do but try to comfort him.

The hours passed slowly pushing on to the evening and the dreaded night. I took mom home because she couldn't tolerate sitting in the chair any longer. She had to lie down and put her feet up.

I went home and cheerfully told my sons who loved their grandfather like a father that the doctors were helping papaw as best they could. They went to bed without knowing the truth.

I told Sonny that the end was near and that if the

phone rang during the night to let me answer it.

I tossed and turned praying for the relief of sleep, but it wasn't to be.

My mind replayed scenes over and over that I didn't want to see.

I watched dad struggle and gasp trying to suck some life sustaining oxygen into his sick lungs.

My mind wouldn't let me see anything else.

I woke myself several times as I, too, fought to breathe.

Your mind can do some really strange things to you.

The alarm sounded at six o'clock the next morning and Sonny and I went about our normal routine of getting the boys ready for school thankful that dad had made it through the night.

I watched my boys board the school bus, then I went to mom's house to pick her up and drive her to the hospital. When I got there, I found a note that my mother had written telling me that my brother was taking her to stay with dad and that she would see me when I got to the hospital. Lee would drop her off and go back home until it was time for him to go to work. He probably would come by the hospital in the evening to sit a while with dad.

Lee didn't seem to understand or accept the seriousness of dad's fight for life.

I started out again for the hospital with a feeling of urgency. I decided to take a short cut over Rosemount

Road to get there faster. When I reached the steep hill that differentiated Rosemount Road from any other road in the area, my car died. It was a sign that the need for urgency was gone.

"What am I going to do now?" I cried as I gazed at the nearby houses searching for a sign of life.

I let the car roll backwards until I could get it off the road, then I went in search of a telephone.

"Lee, I need help. My car quit and I need to get to the hospital," I told him when he answered his telephone.

I thanked God that he was still home and not on his way to work.

"Where are you, sis?"

"I'm at the foot of Rosemount Hill, Twin Valley side. Come take me to the hospital," I pleaded. "I've got to get there."

"Okay, I'm on my way. The hospital called a few seconds ago and said we should get there right now."

I hung up the telephone without even saying goodbye to my brother. I thanked the nice lady who let me use her telephone and I walked to my car where I sat and stared out the window at nothing.

I couldn't see the beauty of the valley that was spread before my eyes. I couldn't see the trees starting to turn different shades of red and yellows with multitudes of rust thrown in for good measure. I couldn't see any of the beauty God had painted on this picture of life. I saw only the dark, sad things implanted in my mind.

I remembered long ago when my grandmother died, dad's mom, how hard dad had taken her death. That was the only time I ever saw my dad cry.

I again remembered what dad had said when we were all sitting in the car as he was driving us home after the funeral. He was talking to mom, but my brother and I were sitting really still in the back seat. We knew not to cause any trouble, that time.

Dad told mom that grandma died of bone cancer, among other problems, and that bone cancer would also kill him.

He was right. He had bone cancer, lung cancer, stomach cancer, and then the doctors stopped looking.

The lung cancer was going to end his life.

Such a horrible way to die.

I could only see the dark, bleak world of pain I was feeling in my heart.

I could feel the hole forming inside my heart where dad's love used to be.

How was I going to live with that hole in my heart?

I didn't notice that Lee's car had pulled up behind mine. I didn't see him get out and it wasn't until he pecked on my window that I acknowledged his presence.

I exited my car, not bothering to lock it, and shuffled to the passenger side of Lee's car. I climbed in without a word passing between us. We rode the remaining three miles in complete and welcomed silence.

I knew we were too late. My heart told me that part of it was dead and gone and would never be refilled again with the love that would be missing.

When we got to dad's room, mom was standing outside his room, crying softly, waiting for us to help her.

I told her to wait a moment and I went in and told him the only thing I could think of as I leaned over the side of the bed to kiss his cheek.

"I love you, Dad, and I love your old, white, picket fence."

The next day or two were a blur of memories that try to hide from my conscious mind.

I remembered talking to mom about what dad should be dressed in when he was laid to rest.

I thought he should be buried in a set of his green work clothes that he wore daily. You saw him in nothing else unless he had a doctor's appointment at which time he would wear the shirt with the white background with tiny blue designs and light blue pin stripes.

Mom chose the white shirt with blue stripes and his only pair of dress slacks.

I wanted the green work clothes but I didn't press the issue.

The last time I saw dad he was wearing that white shirt with tiny blue designs and blue pin stripes. Then they closed the lid on the coffin.

I didn't cry at the funeral I had not cried at the funeral home where he was out on display for all of the relatives and friends to see.

I cried at home when no one was around to see how weak I was.

When I woke up from my memory, I was crying again for the loss of my dad. I missed him so much.

I pulled the quilt close to me so I could see the piece of fabric that had spawned that memory. I couldn't find it anywhere. Nothing I saw came close to what the fabric of dad's shirt had looked like.

"One more night," I mumbled as I sadly crawled from bed. "I'll give it one more night and if the night memories continue, I'm putting this quilt away for good."

CHAPTER 19

THE LITTLE WHITE CHURCH

There was a fabric block of sky blue containing the figure of a small white church with a pointed steeple. It looked like the little white church of Twin Valley

Mom and dad wouldn't go to the little white church, but I did. I didn't want to go to hell and burn forever in those fires.

I would even go to the little white church on Wednesday night and Sunday night if mom and dad would let me. I knew I wasn't going to burn in those hell fires because I went to the little white church.

Dad didn't stop me. He let me get up early each Sunday morning, put on the best dress I could find, and walk out the door with my Bible in my hand.

"That place is full of self-righteous sinners that say they are God-fearing Christians," said my dad one day when I asked him why he didn't attend the little white church. I didn't want him to burn in hell.

"Mom, why don't you and dad go to the little white church?"

"I don't go because your daddy doesn't go. I'm a Methodist and that little white church isn't. Now, don't ask me any more about it," she said sternly.

I knew they were both going to burn in the hell fires.

Reverend Burton was a stocky man of average height with a shiny bald head. He was old. He had to be at least fifty years old.

Mrs. Burton was almost as tall as the mister and she was as round as she was tall. She had a round face that didn't always wear a smile. She could be downright mean looking when she wanted to be.

Mrs. Payne, a really, really old lady with gray curly hair and golden wire-rimmed glasses was one of the Sunday school teachers. She was the one who taught the class I was in each and every Sunday.

Shirley Payne, Mrs. Payne's niece, was the choir director. She was young, just barely out of high school, and quite the looker in a pinched sort of way. The only real fault with Shirley was that she was such a scaredy-cat and everybody knew it.

Easter was coming and I was excited about the extra candy and colored eggs that I would get.

I wasn't excited about going to the little white church on Easter morning.

They would all be decked out in their new Easter finery;

everybody, from the old folks to the babies. I would be able to see the tiny, little holes in the fabric, usually the sleeves, where the price tags were removed.

They would be wearing shoes that were brand spanking new, so new that they would slip and slide on the concrete steps if the wearers weren't careful.

I would be dressed in the same old dress my mother made for me. On my feet would be my school shoes because that's all I had.

Dad had been laid off from his railroad job several months earlier and he was traveling back and forth between home and Indiana where he found a new job.

We had been living on bologna sandwiches and fried chicken for months on end because that was all we could afford. We wouldn't have had that if Mr. and Mrs. Frazier hadn't given dad credit at the grocery store.

Dad wouldn't go to the place where they gave poor people free food. He did it once and that was enough. His pride couldn't handle it again.

I remember that day as one full of excitement. We all piled into the car. My brother and I were in the back seat trying to behave; at least, I was trying. Many times Lee would reach across the seat to punch me and I didn't yell until I couldn't stand the pain anymore.

"Stop hitting me, Lee," I screeched.

"I ain't doing nothing," he said as he held his hands clasped together on his lap.

"Don't whine, Ellen," said dad because he hadn't caught Lee in the act of punching me.

"He keeps hitting me," I said in my own defense.

"Shut up now or we're turning around and going home," dad growled.

We were both quiet. When dad made threats, he carried them out.

I knew from the tone of his voice he wasn't happy.

When we arrived at the food distribution point, dad made us all stay in the car while he went to pick up the box of goods. In the box was commodity peanut butter, cheese, butter, and the like.

I expected lots and lots of food and surprises. What we got was one small brown corrugated box containing a few nondescript cans.

"Ellen, you'll be in Sunday school next Sunday, won't you?"

"No, I don't think so."

"Why not?" probed Mrs. Burton.

"I can't be here, that's all."

"Are you going somewhere with your mom and dad?"

"No ma'am."

"I want you to sing a song for the church service. Can you do that for me?" she asked with a smile.

I wanted to tell her yes because I loved to sing. It still made me nervous to stand up in front of a lot of people, but I did it anyway. Once I got past the first couple of notes of the song, my nerves would settle down and I could do what I liked to do better than anything else.

Quilted Memories

"No, I can't be here on Easter Sunday," I said as I fought the tears that were lingering behind my words.

"Ellen, what's wrong?"

"Everybody will be wearing new Easter clothes, walking around showing off how much money they had to spend. I won't have anything new. I'm not coming to the little white church," I explained between the sobs.

The new dress wasn't important to Mrs. Burton, but it was so very, very important to me.

I was laughed at and made fun of because of the clothes I wore. They were always hand-me-downs or home made by my mother. I didn't think I could stand another special day of the sniggering and laughing at my expense.

"What size do you wear?" she asked as she looked me up and down.

"I don't know. My clothes don't usually have any sizes on the labels because they don't have labels. They have either been cut off or washed so much that the print has faded or they don't have any at all because they were home made."

Mrs. Burton bought me a new dress that I proudly wore to the little white church on Easter Sunday with my cleaned and polished school shoes. I stood straight and tall while I sang the song "Beyond the Sunset" in front of the entire congregation.

Reverend and Mrs. Burton left the little white church after Easter Sunday when Reverend Burton announced that he was retiring. I never saw the Burtons again after that announcement. I wondered if they really wanted to leave. I didn't think it was their choice but I didn't know for sure.

The next minister to take over the pulpit was Noel Burton,

Reverend Burton's nephew.

Noel Burton had two major malfunctions as far as leading the flock of the little white church of Twin Valley was concerned.

His first fault was his youth. Many of the old fogies attending the little white church of Twin Valley could not imagine a young man without sin.

His second fault was being single. Definitely, by all that was holy, the old fogies believed an unmarried man could not be without sin.

It was getting on in time to the end of October with Halloween being right around the corner.

I was twelve and not a leader of the group of kids that were in my Sunday school class. I wasn't always a follower either. If I didn't agree with what they were doing, I went my own way. I didn't want to cause any trouble or make trouble for myself.

At Sunday school, the boys were planning something. You could tell from the eye glints and the hands covering the mouths as they whispered to each other.

"What do you think they're going to do?" my girlfriend and classmate whispered to me during church service.

"I don't know, but I would love to hide and watch," I whispered back to her as I tried to ignore the shushing I was getting from the adults.

Saturday was the day before Halloween. The boys in the neighborhood and in my Sunday school class were known for causing mischief.

Rumors had been flying around the area about how some boys had painted a cow green and it died. Another time, a tree had been chopped down and allowed to fall across the paved road blocking traffic for hours. One time they knocked over outhouses. There was a man sitting in one of the outhouses when it was knocked over. He sure was a mess when he finally crawled out of the hole.

The usual windows being soaped, cars being egged, and corn being tossed always happened. It was part of the rural Halloween ritual.

Nothing happened Saturday morning so I was expecting the event to take place Saturday night. I couldn't sneak out of the house to watch so I'm glad nothing happened Saturday night.

The time had changed from daylight savings to standard so it was dark when the church service would begin Sunday night.

The dew covered the grass causing my world to be wet and cold. I pulled at my sweater trying to make it feel warmer.

"I'm not moving from this place," I mumbled as I tried to convince myself that I should stay until the bitter end. "Why didn't I wear a coat?"

The coldness that would creep into my bones had not crossed my mind as I secreted myself away into my hiding place while there was still enough light to see. The late autumn day had been in the seventies and I forgot that the temperature zoomed to the forties at night.

I was hiding beneath the wooden steps that were located at the back of the church. Those steps had been built because the fire inspector said they were needed in case there was an emergency so people wouldn't run over each other trying to get out the front door. The steps weren't used much. Most of the congregation didn't know they existed, which was a good thing, because it meant there had been no emergencies.

It was dark and cold under the steps and I was crunched up and uncomfortable.

"How much longer?" I whispered to no one because I was alone.

As if in response to my question, I heard voices, distant voices.

"Oh God, they're coming."

The volume of the voices grew louder.

"They're almost here."

I hunkered down waiting, hoping not be attacked by the spiders and bugs I knew were crawling all over my body.

Suddenly, it was quiet. No voices were rumbling along the tarmac. They must have disappeared into one of the houses along the road. I hadn't heard or seen a vehicle of any kind so they must have stopped at one of the houses. I would have to wait longer in the bug-infested confines beneath the wooden steps. I was going to stay beneath those steps until I discovered the truth.

"You can see him walking up the church steps just before Halloween," said Terry in a conspiratorial whisper.

"Who?"

"Old man Ezra Hudson."

"Who was he? I've never heard of an Ezra Hudson."

"He used to own the land that the church is built on. They say he wants it back – the land, I mean."

"Who is they?" asked a skeptical Bobby.

"I don't know. People who live around here, old people."

"Why is he still hanging around? How old is this guy?"

"Ezra Hudson is dead, Bobby. He's been dead for over a hundred years."

"You're kidding?"

"No, I'm not."

"Have you ever seen him?"

"No, I've never really wanted to see a ghost, especially a mean son-of-a-gun like Ezra Hudson was supposed to be."

The conversation stopped suddenly when the young men discovered that I was listening.

"Back off, Ellen. Me and Bobby are having a private talk."

"Sure, Terry. I didn't hear anything anyway."

I went to my history class but had a hard time trying to concentrate on the different stages of development for prehistoric man.

That stolen information from a conversation overheard was the reason I was sitting beneath the steps in the middle of the night.

"Do you think she believed me?" asked Terry.

"Every bit of it. You could see it in her eyes," answered Bobby as they both smiled about what they had done.

"Tell me why we're doing this, Bobby?"

"Because it's fun to pick on her. Everybody does it. She's so stupid. She believes anything you tell her."

"Yeah, right, I forgot," said Terry in a quiet tone.

Now, I was sitting under some nasty, dirty steps, freezing cold, waiting for a ghost to appear.

"Am I stupid, or what?" I asked myself as I moved forward a little so I could change positions and get a better look down the road.

It was a dark, dark night. The full moon that had shown brightly a few minutes earlier was completely covered by slow moving, heavy, dark, clouds.

I was hearing sounds, strange sounds.

I looked through the step treads towards the area where the one and only street light was located.

"That's where it came from," I whispered to my lonesome self.

I strained as I tried to close out the familiar, everyday sounds that were part of the background noise. I heard the snap of the oil furnace as it started to run, warming up the empty church. I heard distant car doors slamming and faint tinkling of television sets. Someone must really be hard of hearing for me to hear the televisions.

It was a dragging sound, like something heavy being pulled across the pavement up near the street light. I kept my steady gaze at the area beneath the street light. It seemed to be a spot or circle of light that was surrounded by total darkness.

I could hear the dragging but I couldn't see who was doing it. What was it? What was so heavy that it had to be dragged, not carried, along the pavement?

I inched forward trying to force my eyes to see what obviously couldn't be seen. I had to move out from under the steps. I wasn't going to be able to figure out what was going on if I didn't crawl from the confining space.

I had to lower my head and get down on my knees to get from beneath the steps. While I was twisting and contorting my body around, the dragging sounds ceased.

I was standing next to the steps brushing the spider webs from my hair when I heard voices.

"Throw it up over the limb," said a masculine sounding voice in a harsh whisper.

"I'm trying to. Shut up already."

I didn't move away from the steps. I didn't want to be seen by those who were out in the dark of night.

"The rope is long enough so I'm going to drop it all the way to the ground. I'll tie it off on the bridge railing over here and then we can finish the job."

I could hear the footsteps pounding the pavement as the person who has been speaking ran to a different location.

"Grab that noose."

"Okay, okay, I've got it."

"Wrap it around that tree over there. I think I hear a car coming. Hide, for God's sake. Get out of sight, now."

"I don't see a car."

"It must have turned off on one of the side roads. Let's get this finished."

My eyes widened with fear. What were they doing? Why were they hiding from passing cars?

"Get the body."

"I need some help. He's awfully heavy."

"Okay, okay, quit your whining."

"I'll hold him up so you can put the noose around his neck."

They were hanging somebody.

Why were they doing that? In the middle of the street? Right under a street light? Why?

"It's going to take both of us pulling to get the body in the air. I want it all the way up swinging in the breeze directly under the street light for all the world to see, especially Ellen."

Suddenly I knew the voices.

Payback was going to be had.

I knew about the broken lock on the window that opened into the basement of the church. I got down on my hands and knees, gently pushed against the window, and crawled inside the basement of the church. I found the candle and matches that were always left in the basement for emergencies when the lights went out.

I lit the candle and made my way to the first floor of the church.   I opened the front door slightly so I could see that Bobby and Terry were still messing with their hanging man.

I ran to the church organ and played a really loud chord that could be heard all the way down the street. Then I ran back to the front door of the church where the bell pull for the church bell was located and quickly yanked the bell into life.

I snapped the front door lock and pulled it closed behind me as I left the church leaving a flickering candle in the window.

Again, I ran to the steps where I would hide just in case

someone wanted to do any investigating.

"What was that? There's someone over at the church. Look, Bobby, there's some kind of light over there. See!" said Terry as he pointed towards the church.

"Don't lie to me, Terry, there's no one over there," said Bobby as he worked with the rope he was trying to tie down so the body wouldn't come crashing to the ground scattering the straw stuffing all over kingdom come.

"Look, Bobby. Look!"

Bobby turned his head towards the church just as the church organ sounded.

"Who did that?" asked Bobby as his eyes widened in terror.

"Nobody. There are no cars parked in front or lights on in the church except that one over there flickering. It must be a candle."

"Somebody has to be in there. Somebody is just trying to scare us."

"Well, they're doing a pretty good job of it," whined Terry.

The bells started ringing and a strange masculine but wavy voice shouted out, "I want my land back. Give me my land."

Bobby and Terry took off running while I laughed until tears streamed down my cheeks.

At school the next day, I smiled at Bobby and Terry each time I passed them in the halls.

"Hey, Ellen," shouted Bobby, "were you out by the church last night?"

"Why would you ask that?"

"Just wondering. You heard about the commotion didn't you?"

"Are you talking about the hanging man? I know you and Terry did that. I saw you guys dragging the body over to the light."

"No, I'm not talking about that."

"You mean the bells ringing? Must have been somebody pulling a Halloween prank. You didn't do it, did you?"

"Who me?" asked Bobby as he feigned surprise.

"Did anything else happen?" I probed.

"Terry said he heard old man Ezra Hudson shouting about wanting his land back."

"Oh, really? I didn't know that," I said as I puzzled over what he was saying.

I hadn't heard old man Ezra Hudson and I had been standing right there.

That same night of the Halloween fracas, Shirley Payne lived within walking distance of the little white church. There was a streetlight in front of Shirley's house. It was one of the two streetlights in Twin Valley with the second one being in front of little white church. She walked out the front door of her house where she lived with her mother, and nearly fell as her feet slid on the hard kernels of corn that had been tossed at her house. She glanced at the windows of the door and those facing the front of the house and saw that they were nearly obscured with soap.

She was so angry that she was nearly foaming at the mouth. Her thin body was shaking and her jaw was clinching.

She continued to walk away from her porch when she looked

up and saw the body hanging from the streetlight. The boys had already left the scene running as fast as they could from old man Hudson.

It was a man, an average built man, swinging in the wind as he was suspended from a rope with a noose around his neck. This was the handiwork of the running boys.

I was sitting on the top step of the steps leading up to the front door of the little white church. I saw it all happen before my very own eyes. I didn't have to hide and watch.

Shirley let out a scream loud enough to wake the dead, she wobbled around weakly, and then she collapsed to the ground.

Noel Burton was standing at the bottom of the steps of the little white church. He had driven into the parking lot and was about to climb the steps when he heard the scream.

He took off running towards the scream as did I. He gingerly placed his hands beneath Shirley's unconscious body. He lifted her up and took her inside the house while Shirley's mother held the door open for him.

He had seen the body suspended from the rope but he paid no mind to it. After all, it was Halloween.

Shirley's mother told Noel to go on to the little white church to attend his meeting and she would look after Shirley.

Noel had been linked with Shirley in the eyes of the congregation because she, too, was unmarried.

Shirley never did return to the little white church of Twin Valley. The rumors flew around hot and heavy about her having been pregnant by Noel and losing the baby the night she fainted.

None of the tales were true about the baby. She had dated

Noel but I didn't think he was stupid enough to lose his job over crazy Shirley.

None of the boys confessed to hanging the straw-filled dummy from the streetlight. I surely wasn't going to tell on them even though I had watched the whole scene as it was taking place. This fat female was having enough trouble with making friends and trying to get along with everybody. I didn't want a new crop of enemies.

My girlfriend and I were getting to the age where we were noticing males. Noel was free, white, and over twenty-one. Noel, especially, was a male.

I wasn't boy crazy because I had been made fun of by too many of those boy monsters because I was overweight.

The girls with the budding breasts and who were proud owners of menstrual cycles were strutting their stuff in front of Noel.

He was fired soon after the girls started strutting because he was a free, white, over twenty-one male. Nothing was done about the strutters. You couldn't fire them.

In my thirteenth year, my dad packed us up and moved us two hundred and fifty miles away. Before I left I had become a baptized member of the little white church of Twin Valley.

Four years later, after I graduated from high school, I wrote to the little white church of Twin Valley and asked for the Bible that I would have received when I graduated from high school if I were still living in Twin Valley.

They sent me my beautiful white Bible with my name printed on the lower part of the front cover in gold letters to match the gold edged pages.

I was so very proud of that Bible and vowed that I would return to that church someday because that was where I belonged.

I had every reason to believe that when and if I ever returned to Twin Valley I would be readily accepted back into the fold to become a permanent member of the flock.

Twenty years after my family moved away, I returned to Twin Valley to live in the same house that my mom and dad had kept up and maintained for all of those years.

When I returned, I had two young sons in tow who had chosen, through the legal system, to carry my maiden name that I returned to after my divorce and the name of their grandfather whom they adored.

I was not invited back to the church where I was baptized. No one knocked on my door welcoming me back into the fold.

I asked my neighbor about what was going on at that little white church.

"Your boys have the same name you had when you left here."

"Yes, so what?" I said as I paused while a rush of embarrassment and anger spread through my body. "They don't think my sons are legitimate, do they? What about you? What do you think?" I asked angrily.

"I don't know, Ellen. They do have your dad's name and your birth name."

"Kathy, I was married to the father of my sons. I changed their names to their grandfather's name at their request through the court system; then, I changed mine. I don't think I need to explain this to anyone, do you?"

"Well, you know how people talk. They don't want divorced people attending their little white church either. To tell you the truth, that's why I don't go there. I'm divorced, too," she mumbled in embarrassment.

I didn't feel that the little white church of Twin Valley deserved an explanation and I certainly wasn't going to give them one. I could recall no time when the right to make judgments about any fellow man or woman was given solely to the little white church of Twin Valley.

During the twenty years I was away from that little white church, I discovered what my dad had told me was true.

"That place is full of self-righteous sinners."

I guess I was doomed to burn in the fires of hell because I wasn't going back to the little white church of Twin Valley where the hearts of the congregation were black. I would find a place where they accepted real people into their fold. I wanted to go where I wasn't judged as evil before they bothered to find the truth.

CHAPTER 20

LUNCH HOUR WEDDING

A quilt block be-speckled with multicolored hearts made my mind wander to the only living man left in my small world- Sonny.

I watched him as he was sitting on one of those extremely uncomfortable blue chairs in the waiting room. There was something about him, something I just couldn't put my finger on, that made me sneak a peek every time I raised my head from staring at my typewriter.

He had a pleasant face, a medium build, and medium blonde hair of which a lock or two kept falling forward forcing him to brush it back.

He had asked to see Mr. Burton, my boss, and a damn good attorney, about filing for a divorce. As sad as the idea of divorce should seem to anyone, inwardly I was happy about the thought that he would be available.

He was talking to another man who had come into the

lobby with him. The other man, who turned out to be Sonny's brother, Don, was unhappy about not being able to drink his can of beer that was sitting in the car getting warm. Don fidgeted and squirmed in his chair much like an impatient child.

I don't think either one of them saw me sneaking peeks, at least, I hoped they didn't.

Don stood up and angrily told Sonny, by whom I was mesmerized, that he would be waiting in the car.

"Good riddance. You're drunk," I heard Sonny whisper as Don walked out of the room.

"Do you know how much longer it will be before I can talk to Mr. Burton?" he asked as he stood in front of my desk.

"I'm sorry, sir, but Mr. Burton is with another client. It shouldn't be much longer," I said as kindly as I could because I knew that people hated to wait.

"My name is Sonny."

"My name is Ellen. Would you like to look at a magazine? I'll get one for you if you like?" I asked as I tried to get him to talk to me.

A few moments later I heard Mr. Burton come to the doorway, walking the client with whom he had been speaking through the lobby and holding the door for him as the client exited the room. He gently closed the door and looked at Sonny.

"Are you here to see me?" he asked Sonny.

"If you're Mr. Burton? Yes sir, I'm here to see you."

"Come on in the office. We'll get you started."

I watched Sonny and Mr. Burton leave the reception area. My mind was running in overdrive. How was I going to get to know Sonny? There was just something about him.

Several days passed before I saw Sonny again. I had to call him and schedule an appointment for him to sign the divorce papers before they were filed in court. At the very least, I had his telephone number even if I was too old-fashioned to use it for my own purposes. To my way of thinking, the man should make the first move.

When he entered the lobby for his newly scheduled appointment, his face lit up with sunshine when he said hello to me. His bright, blue eyes sparkled with merriment accented by fine lines of age that formed a starburst of happiness. His smile matched his eyes.

I know I turned every shade of red as I wondered if he knew how hard I had been concentrating on getting him to ask me out for a date.

I knew he had four children ranging in ages from elementary school to high school, but I also had two boys in middle school.

Mr. Burton took Sonny into his office right away and I didn't get a chance to talk with him. On his way past my desk and out the door, Sonny whispered for me to call him. I nodded in acknowledgment of his request.

"I can't call Sonny," I told myself as I thought about his

request.

I was daydreaming about what to do next when the telephone rang and my oldest son was on the line.

"Mom, we have snakes under the house!" he said excitedly.

"What?"

"Mrs. Johnson said she saw a great, big, old copperhead crawl under our house," he explained.

"You and Aaron stay in the house, Eddy, and don't go to the back yard. I'll see if anyone knows how to get rid of snakes. Okay?"

"All right, but do something, will you?" he pleaded.

No one was in the office for me to ask so I called Sonny.

"Do you know how to get rid of snakes?" I asked when Sonny came to the telephone.

"What? Snakes? Who is this?" he sputtered into the receiver.

"This is Ellen," I explained. "You and I spoke to each other in Attorney Burton's Office. Don't you remember me?" I said as my voice began to trail off and fade away.

"Sure, you're Mr. Burton's secretary. How are you?" he asked in a not-too-confident tone.

"Never mind," I said quietly. "I'll find out from someone else. I'll just say goodbye and we can forget this conversation ever happened," I said as I tried to end the phone call without embarrassing myself any further.

"No...no...please don't hang up. I'm glad you called. Where are the snakes?"

We talked for several minutes and he made a date to come to my house to investigate my snake problem.

****

"Ellen, I made the last payment on our rings today. See, here's the receipt," said Sonny as he proudly displayed the small, yellow receipt with 'PAID IN FULL" written in bold letters across it.

"Where are they?"

"Right here," he said as he plunged his hand into his jacket extracting the blue, velvet-lined box. "When can we get married?"

"Soon, real soon."

"What about next week?"

"Okay, but we've got to buy our license and then we have to wait three days."

"It won't be anything fancy. Nothing like what you're entitled to," Sonny whispered apologetically.

"It doesn't have to be fancy, Honey. We love each other and that's all we need."

"Are you going to take any time off work?"

"I can't. Mr. Burton is going to be out of town for about a month, and I have to help him tie up loose ends before he leaves.

You know what a busy lawyer he is," I answered sadly.

"What are we going to do?" Sonny asked guessing that the wedding was going to be delayed again.

"We'll get our marriage license Monday during the lunch hour. Then, we'll drive five miles to New Boston to be married by the mayor on Friday during the lunch hour. I've already checked with the mayor's office."

We had been planning to get married for three months. In August we had put a small down payment on our rings having decided to be married on September 16th which was the 39th wedding anniversary of my parents.

A couple of days after the down payment was made, I was told that my father had cancer and would only have a few months to live.

Our marriage plans were completely halted when my father's health moved quickly from bad to worse. The money that was intended to pay for the rings was used for other expenses and the bedside vigil took precedence over the frivolity of wedding preparations.

On September 16th, the day Sonny and I had planned to be married, my father succumbed to cancer.

Almost a month later, we were excited again about being able to get married. We had decided to tell no one just in case something else happened to force us to change our plans again.

"Ellen?"

"Sonny, what's the matter? Why aren't you on your way here to pick me up?"

"The car won't start."

Quilted Memories

"Oh."

"What do you want me to do now?"

"Just get it fixed. We'll go tomorrow. There will still be enough time. Don't worry, okay? Just get the car fixed."

I went through the remainder of Monday at work like a lost soul. Even though I had encouraged Sonny with cheerful words, I was so afraid something else would go wrong.

Tuesday was the day to get the license.

Sonny picked me up and we drove the five miles to New Boston, completed the necessary paperwork, grabbed a quick sandwich, and I returned to work.

"Where'd you go for lunch?" asked Thelma.

"We grabbed a hamburger and drove around for a while."

"Oh, I thought you might have done something different," added Thelma as she was leaving the room.

I smiled and went about my work. I was so happy about getting married, finally, that I wanted to share the feeling with the world.

My happy feeling was replaced with nervous anticipation that caused my mind to jump around, and concentration on work became a difficult task. Sleeping that night was even harder to do. My mind had covered every possible mishap from the car not starting again to my having a heart attack.

When the alarm rang Friday morning, I jumped out of bed checking to see that I was not having chest pains.

I picked out one of my nicer outfits to wear keeping in mind that I still had to go to work.

I called Sonny so I could hear his voice and make sure everything was going smoothly so far.

"Hi, honey," I said into the receiver after I heard his sleepy hello.

"Is there anything wrong, Ellen?" he asked worriedly.

"No, everything is fine. Everything is perfect. I just wanted to hear your voice and tell you that I love you."

"I love you, too."

"I'll see you at noon. I love you, Sonny."

"Love you, too."

I replaced the telephone receiver and went to my car.

"Nellie, don't fail me now," I prayed as I turned the ignition key to start my car. When the engine roared to life I was relieved. Now, my only worry was that Sonny's car wouldn't start.

"Ellen, you want to go to lunch with Teresa and me?" asked Thelma.

"No, I can't. Sonny is picking me up."

"Again? Where are you going this time?"

"New Boston."

"You going to the steak house?" probed Thelma.

"Yes, I may be a little late. Will you cover for me?" I answered hoping Thelma would end the inquisition.

"Sure, no problem. Have a good lunch," she said as I walked out the door.

When Sonny pulled to the curb in front of the building, I jumped into the car and kissed him before he had a chance to say hello.

We were on our way.

At the mayor's office, we waited a few minutes while the mayor, who was also a minister, readied himself for the short service.

The actual marriage ceremony took only five minutes and the pep talk issued by the mayor was short and sweet.

When Sonny and I left the mayor's office, we were husband and wife. We were each wearing a beautiful, golden, wedding band that bound us together forever.

"Sonny, we've got to stop at the steak house," I giggled.

"Why? We don't have time to eat. You have to get back to work."

"I know, but I told Thelma that was where I was going and I want to make sure it wasn't a lie. All I want to do is walk through the front door then turn around and leave."

"You're crazy, Ellen."

"No, honey, just honest."

When I arrived at work, I was about fifteen minutes late.

"Did you have a good lunch?" questioned Thelma.

"Sure did," I replied as I flagrantly waved my left hand in front of Thelma.

"What's that?"

"What?"

"On your left hand?"

"That's my wedding band. I just got married."

"You're kidding?"

"No, I'm now Mrs. Sonny Hoagland and the happiest woman alive."

The lunch hour wedding occurred over twenty years ago and Sonny and I remain together but not for the love of snakes.

On November 3, 2008, my beloved Sonny passed away. I miss him so much.

CHAPTER 21

HOT SUN – HOT TEMPERS

It was hot, so very hot, the quilt was covering me from head to toe. It was tucked in around me not allowing any cold air to infiltrate. I wandered into another memory.

The sun was just coming over the trailer park. I blinked my eyes as I tried to clear away the fog from sleep. The air was cool now, but, give it an hour or two, the metal cracker box that we lived in would turn into a sauna.

We had arrived home yesterday afternoon during the strongest heat of the day from our little excursion to St. Albans to visit my Aunt Mintha. Now the fun and joy of vacationing and visiting was over and I had to face the enormous pile of dirty laundry that would be mounded up on the kitchen floor as it awaited its turn to become the fresh sweet smelling clothes to be worn tomorrow and the next day and the next until the mound accumulated again.

It was Saturday morning. At least, I had Saturday and Sunday before I had to return to the grind of processing mortgage loan applications at the bank. Thank goodness the bank was air conditioned. That was the only thing that made going to work pleasurable.

I searched for a clean pair of shorts and a tee shirt so I could tackle the day head-on and get the dreaded duties underway before the sun rose high in the sky and sapped all my strength and energy away in this metal coffin.

"Mrs. Hoagland, are you home?" said a female voice as a fist pounded loudly at my front door.

Why in the world would anybody be pounding on my front door at seven in the morning? Is there some kind of emergency? If so, it doesn't involve my family. I'm the only person awake, or at least I was the only one, until the pounding started.

"Who is it?" I shouted as I worked the locks so I could open the heavy metal door.

"Mrs. Jennings. I live two trailers over from you. I need to talk to you about your kid."

Finally I had the door open and was staring into the eyes of a very angry woman.

"What's your problem?" I snapped at her so she wouldn't be the only angry person in the confrontation.

"Your kid, the little blonde one, he's my problem. He's going to be your problem, too. That's for sure."

"That kid has a name; Aaron is his name. Now what about Aaron?" I said as I held tightly to the handle to the storm door. I didn't want her barging into my space and getting physical.

"A couple of nights ago, Thursday, that's when I saw him, he broke the glass out of my brand new storm door that I just bought

215

and hadn't had a chance to get anybody to hang it into place. I had it leaning up against my trailer. I saw that mean little kid of yours, the blonde headed one, jumping up and down breaking out the glass in the door. I saw him with my own two eyes," she said as she gestured toward her face.

I looked at her and saw for myself that she was totally and completely crazy. I held onto the door handle a little tighter.

"You're crazy, what did you say your name was?"

"Jennings is my name and why don't you step outside here and we'll see who is crazy?" she sputtered as her eyes sparkled with anger when she tossed back her hair with a quick nod of her head.

"Mrs. Jennings, my son did not break your door," I could feel the hackles rising up on my back.

"I seen him with my own two eyes," she shouted back at me.

"I don't doubt that you saw somebody do it, but it wasn't Aaron," I spoke forcefully as I clenched my jaw trying to hold back the flood of ugly, nasty words that were filling my brain.

"Yes, I did. It was a blond headed kid. The one that wears the glasses," she said as she stepped as close to the storm door as she could without pressing her face directly up against it.

"Go home, Mrs. Jennings, you're not going to get any money out of me," I said as I started to close the door.

"I'm going to call the law if you don't pay me fifty dollars so I can get another door. You hear me? I want fifty dollars from you or I will call the law."

"Go ahead, call the law. I can't wait to tell them that Aaron wasn't even in this state on Thursday. Now, get out of here and don't be bothering me anymore," I said as I slammed the door in her face.

I took a deep breath and started to walk towards the kitchen to tackle the waiting laundry.

Suddenly there was a loud knock at my back door. I grabbed a broom as I walked through the kitchen and struggled with the lock on the back door.

"Ellen, your oldest boy tried to set fire to my trailer."

"I think this whole place has gone nuts!" I shouted at John who was my backside neighbor. My trailer back end sat across from his trailer back end.

"When, John? When was this supposed to have happened?" I snarled.

"Yesterday evening, I saw you guys get home and unload your car. Then, about an hour later I smelled smoke. That's when I saw your oldest boy, the one with the dark hair, running between the trailers."

"He never left the trailer after we got home yesterday, John. I know for a fact that he never left the house. I was sitting in the living room watching television. It was too hot to do anything else. There is no way he could slip out of the house without me seeing him."

"I'm going to call the sheriff and report him as an arsonist."

"Let me see the proof, John. Show me the ashes."

John led the way to a small pile of rubble that had been pulled from beneath his trailer while it had been burning. Someone actually did try to burn his place down, but It wasn't Eddy that did it.

"John, you don't have very many friends in this trailer park because you're so hard to get along with. Why would you think Eddy would try to burn you out?"

"He told me he would get even with me someday for cutting down his marijuana plants. Those are illegal, you know. I should have called the law then," he said as anger reddened his long, skinny face.

"I knew what those plants were, John. They were in flower pots and back behind the house. He carried those plants in and out every day. He hid them in his closet when they were in the trailer. I wasn't going to let him do anything with them except let them grow for a while. It gave him something to do. He thought he was doing something really bad. He thought he was putting something over on his mother by telling me they were tomato plants. I thought it was funny. I don't blame him for being mad at you, John. You should have talked to me before you cut them down."

"I saw him running away. It was him, all right."

"Did you see his face?"

"No, just the back of his head."

"Then, you didn't actually see who it was, did you?"

"I know it was him and I'm calling the sheriff."

"Go right ahead, John. I'll be waiting right here in this house and so will my boys."

I started the laundry and kept myself busy as I awaited the arrival of the sheriff after being summon by Mrs. Jennings who said Aaron broke her door and John who swore that Eddy tried to burn down his house.

The sheriff didn't arrive to drag me off for being a bad mother that day or any day after that for the destruction my boys were supposed to have done. As a matter of fact, the kid who had just moved out of the trailer park was the one who confessed to his mother who told John that he was the one who tried to burn John's trailer down and that he was sorry that the fire went out and he didn't get the job done. Must have been some real animosity there but I didn't know anything about that.

As far as Mrs. Jennings was concerned, I don't believe she ever had a new storm door. I think she was just trying to get some money out of me and I wasn't willing to cooperate.

The boys and I climbed into the car and went hunting for a couple of air conditioners that afternoon. I was going to put a unit on each end of the trailer and at least keep our sun heated tempers under control. There wasn't anything I could do for the other hot heads in the trailer park.

CHAPTER 22

WHITE-HAIRED GRANDPA

Again, white filled my dreams, the soft white of clouds and angel wings.

He was a tall man being well over six feet. This was tall in my family. Dad was only about 5'7", mom was only 5'4", Lee the next tallest was 5'11", and I didn't quite make it to 5'2".

It wasn't just his lofty height that made him bigger than life. He had a kind face that made his blue eyes sparkle with warmth. The skin around his eyes was crinkled with laugh lines and his mouth had a natural upturn on each side that made him look like he was always smiling. As wonderful as his blue eyes and the natural smile were, his most striking feature was his full crown of snow white hair.

When my son Eddy wasn't quite two years old, he saw his great grandpa for the first time. Eddy was drawn to the white hair that he wanted to touch and pat like you would stroke an animal.

We had driven from Cleveland, Ohio, to St. Albans, West Virginia, so that we could visit my grandmother's grave. My grandfather had had her grave moved from the hilltop family cemetery in one of the back hollows of West Virginia in which it had originally been placed to a church cemetery in Alum Creek where he would be able to visit the grave much easier in his waning years.

The day was sunny and the sky was the most beautiful shade of blue I had ever seen as we walked through the Alum Creek cemetery looking at the graves of various members of my dad's side of the family.

My tall grandfather, Eddy's great grandfather, was holding the up stretched hand of the tiny, dark haired Eddy walking through the cemetery as if that was the most natural thing for them to do.

The fact that they were complete and total strangers to each other was not evident.

That was the first and the last time Eddy saw his great grandfather.

"When are we going to see my white-haired grandpa again?" asked Eddy several years after meeting his great grandfather for the first and only time.

"Who are you talking about?"

"The grandpa with the white hair?"

"Oh, your great grandpa, is that who you mean?"

"I guess."

"You were so young when you saw him. Are you sure it was him?'

"He's the only man I ever saw with such white hair."

221

"You won't be seeing him again, Eddy. He died a couple of years ago."

"Oh," was his only response.

I smiled as I remembered the image of the tall, straight-backed, great grandfather with the snow white hair walking between the grave markers. His large black, polished shoes and Eddy's tiny sneakers were crushing the blades of bright green grass as he clutched my son's tiny hand in his enormous palm. They both looked as if they were engrossed into the most important conversation of their lives. They were both spilling over will love for each other.

****

The red block represented danger and forced memories about Aaron to the forefront.

"Don't go near that!" I screamed at my son as he wheeled his way towards the kitchen counter and the dangling cord. I jumped up from my seat at the dining table and turned his walker away from the enticement to danger. I lifted the dangling cord to the top of the counter so that he would no longer want to pull on it to find out what was on the other end of the plastic string. I tried to be so careful.

My hands were surrounding the cup of black liquid that had been placed on the table in front of me. I was sharing a moment with a friend in the break room before facing the mounds of paper on our desks in the unfriendly confines of our respective offices. Annie's chattering stopped and I had a free moment to think. My eyes roamed around the small room and stopped at the coffeepot. I stared at the coffeepot cursing its existence. I didn't want to be around that coffeepot, that weapon of child torture. The liquid fire that burned my baby's skin.

Aaron was rolling around in his walker when he spied a dangling cord. Those quick little hands grabbed and pulled before the babysitter had a chance to stop him. Time and time again I had turned his body and walker away from the cord. It didn't occur to me that the babysitter would not watch him as closely as I did.

The burning hot coffee poured over him from his left shoulder down the front of his tiny body.

The red sweater knit romper he was wearing served to only absorb the heat forcing the hot coffee to corrode and burn his tender skin.

I had only moments before walked out the front door with car key in hand to travel to town to pick up my husband and Aaron's father from work. I hadn't pulled the car from the driveway before I saw a screaming babysitter trying to flag me down.

I threw the car into park, left it standing with the engine running and blocking the driveway that served four houses, as I raced into the house to help my screaming baby.

I jerked his new red sweater suit from his wriggling body, wrapped him in my quilt, a blanket was too fuzzy, and handed him to the babysitter to hold. I ran across the driveway where I stuck my head inside the front door of my mom and dad's house.

"Get your pocketbook, mom! Aaron's been hurt?"

It was snowing as I drove to the nearest hospital, with my mother by my side, holding my screaming son.

The roads were slippery because of the thick layer of ice hidden beneath the new fallen snow.

Nothing was going to stop me, my baby was crying in pain from the burning fire of hot liquid.

Quilted Memories

Upon arrival at the emergency room, we were waved past the desk, due to the nature of the injury, and led to a cubicle where we would wait for the arrival of the doctor.

The first person to see Aaron was a nurse who brought in cool gauze pads to place on the burns. I told her what had happened as she helped my son.

The second person to enter the cubicle was a social worker.

"Why did you burn your son?"

I looked at her as I tried to understand the words that had come from her mouth. Suddenly, I realized she was accusing me of hurting Aaron, my baby, my son, on purpose.

I walked towards her in a menacing way and I had no idea what I would do if I, somehow, was near enough to do some damage to her person.

"Get out of here!" I shouted. "My God, I wouldn't burn my son on purpose! It was an accident. So help me, God, it was an accident."

"Some people do hurt their children. I hope you're not one of them," she whispered as she left the cubicle with a look on her face that expressed fear. I'm sure she was afraid for her own well-being if she lingered too long in front of me.

The dark-haired, bearded doctor was patient with Aaron and kind to me. He didn't seem to think I purposely burned my son. Because of the pain and suffering Aaron had to endure, my two year-old son would scream each and every time he saw a man sporting a beard. Aaron seemed to associate the beard and the pain and would let no bearded man near him without screaming.

Thankfully the social worker asked me no more stupid questions. I was afraid of what I might do to her if she got into my face again.

Me? Burn my son with boiling hot coffee? No way would I ever do that!

Aaron healed with only a small permanent scar under his arm to serve as a reminder of the fire damage, even liquid fire, can cause. The only other sign of the accident was a long white patch of skin that would not tan in the summer sun and, of course, the fear of bearded men.

My hatred of social workers faded and eventually I came to realize that she was doing her job to the best of her ability. It didn't matter to her how I felt about the accusations because her goal was to help the poor, defenseless child.

Just as an added note, the coffeepot cord never dangled in my house again.

CHAPTER 23

THE LADDER

The faded denim blue square meant work.

"It is a job that has to be done and I am the one who has to do it. There isn't anyone else around that I can ask that would be able to do the dreaded job. I am going to have to suck it up and just do it, fear or no fear, get on with it and get it done," I said in a pep talk to myself as I rounded up the tools that were necessary to complete the task at hand.

No amount of talking to myself was going to make it any easier for me except that it kept my mind busy along with my hands and feet that were going about their business of gathering paint brushes, rollers, paint, rags, and, of course, the ladder.

The ladder was an extension ladder that would stretch all the way to the top that was equivalent to a two story house. In order for me the do the job as it should be done, the ladder would have to be pulled out to the furthest it could be extended safely.

Why on earth did our mobile home have to be placed in a lot where the back end of the trailer extended out over a sloping hillside? Flat land would have been much nicer and a heck of a lot easier when it came to painting an aging structure.

The thought of climbing up that wobbly, flimsy, aluminum ladder petrified me to the point of tears.

I sat at the foot of the extended aluminum ladder and cried. Fear can do horrible things to a person's mind. It was having a field day with my mind, soul, and body.

I was pretty sure I could trace the beginning of my fear of heights. I was also pretty sure that the fear of heights was never, ever going to go away. All I wanted to do was crawl into a hole in my mind long enough for me to get the peak of the mobile home painted. As I sat there crying, I remembered why I was so afraid of heights.

"Ellen, let's go to the store," whispered my brother as he pulled me to my feet from the sofa I was sitting on as I played with my Tiny Tears doll.

"No, I don't have any money," I whined and pulled back so I could remain on the sofa.

"I do. I did some weed pulling for Mrs. Bainer. She gave me fifty cents. I'll buy you a candy bar. One of those three cent chocolate ones you like," he said as he continued to pull on my arm.

"Go by yourself and get me a candy bar anyway."

"If you don't go with me, you won't get any candy," he taunted.

I had to think about it for a few seconds. It was so hot outside that I really didn't want to leave my position in front of the fan. A candy bar – I hadn't had a candy bar since...I couldn't remember when.

"Okay. Did mommy say we could?"

"Come with me and we'll ask."

"Why didn't you ask already?"

"I wanted you to be with me. I wanted her to see that I was going to take my stupid little sister with me," he said as he led the way from the living room to the kitchen.

"I'm not stupid and I'm not going."

"No candy bar," he said in a taunting whisper.

We stood before my mother staring up at her with pleading expressions on our faces.

"What do you two want?" she asked as she prepared the water to wash the dishes that were piled in the sink.

"Ellen and I want to walk to the store."

"Why?"

"Mrs. Bainer paid me fifty cents for pulling weeds. I want to spend it."

"Are you going to buy Ellen something?"

"Yeah, a candy bar. I already told her I would pay for a candy bar."

"All right, but be careful. You know the teenagers around here speed up and down that road like crazy people. They'll hit you in a minute and keep on driving. Watch your little sister real close. You hear me, Lee?"

"Yeah, mommy. I'll watch her," he said as he pulled an ugly face in my direction.

I hated to go anywhere with my brother because he was a bully, especially if mommy and daddy weren't around to keep tight rein on him.

"Come on, Ellen, let's go."

All ready I regretted my decision.

"Why did you ask me come with you?"

"Because I knew mommy wouldn't let me go to spend money if I didn't spend some of it on you. It's not fair, you know. I worked for that money. You didn't."

"I could."

"You're too little. No one would pay you anything because you can't do anything."

"Yes, I can."

"No, you can't. Now go on, start walking."

I was near tears but I wasn't going to let him see me cry, not when mommy and daddy weren't around to do anything about it.

The store wasn't very far from our house but it was far enough away so that we would disappear from sight and that was what frightened my mother. She wanted us within her line of vision at all times, except when we were in school.

Mommy and daddy were not social people. They had a nodding acquaintance with the neighbors, but they didn't visit, so we weren't allowed to visit. That also meant that others weren't allowed to visit us either.

Mommy did some of the forbidden neighborly things when daddy wasn't home, but she knew he would get mad if he found out about it.

The only playmates my brother and I had during most of our childhood were each other. I learned to play alone. That's when I developed my love for reading. It wasn't fun playing with a bully.

He was pushing me along the road, not really watching for cars or anything.

"Lee, stop a minute, I have a rock in my shoe."

I sat down on the grass at the side of the road and pulled off my old tennis shoe so I could remove the rock.

"Lee, I haven't seen the Springers for a long time. Where are they?"

"Old man Springer died and his wife is living with her daughter. No one's living in the house anymore. I think they're going to sell it."

"To who?"

"I don't know. Let's go take a look around."

"We better not."

"Don't be chicken, Ellen."

"I'm not a chicken. Mommy will get mad."

"I'm not going to tell her. Are you going to be a tattletale? Tattletale, tattletale, Ellen is a tattletale."

"Stop calling me that."

"Then, let's look around."

We started walking toward the house that really didn't look empty. I mean there were still curtains over the windows and furniture in place. So I knew they didn't want anybody prowling around in their belongings.

"I'll stay out front here by the shade trees. You go look around."

"You are such a scaredy cat, Ellen."

"I don't want to get into trouble."

"You won't, nobody will see us."

I followed him as he walked around the Springer house looking for a way inside but he couldn't find one without breaking something and I was dead set against that.

"Put that rock down, Lee. I'll tell on you."

"You'll be telling on yourself because you're with me."

"I know but I won't be the one breaking the window. You will, and I'll tell mommy you did it. She'll tell daddy and you'll get a whipping."

Lee lunged at me like he wanted to break all of my bones in my body but he did throw the rock into the wooded area behind the house.

When we walked back to the front of the house, he started climbing one of the two trees. Not to be out done by my stupid brother, I climbed the second tree. I never gave it any thought that once I climbed up the tree, I would have to climb back down.

We both sat in the separate trees watching the world go by for a few minutes, then it became time to get down.

Lee clambered down the tree in no time. Then it was my turn.

The limb I was perched on wasn't very far from the ground but when I looked down from my position in the tree it looked a mile off of the green grass.

"Come on, Ellen, we've got to get to the store and then get home. Mommy will be looking for us."

"Okay, just a minute," I said in a weak voice.

I started to twist around so I could shimmy down the tree and I froze. Fear had overtaken every part of my body. No way could I will myself to move.

"Let's go, Ellen. We've got to go now," he yelled at me in angry tones.

"I'm afraid."

"Afraid of what?"

"Afraid of falling. I'm afraid of falling," I cried as I held my eyes closed as tight as I could.

"Get out of that tree now," Lee growled.

"I can't."

"If you don't get out now, I'll shove you out," he hissed at me.

"No! Lee, no!" I screamed as I held onto the tree with all of my strength.

I was almost laying down on the limb with my short arms wrapped around the tree as far as I could reach. It would have taken very little effort on Lee's part to knock me to the ground if he could reach me.

He started jumping up and stretching as far as he could with his arms trying to knock me down to the ground below. It probably wouldn't have hurt me if he had succeeded but I wasn't willing to take the chance.

I continued to scream hoping the noise would scare him and that he would stop jumping and pushing at me and go get help.

"Hey, boy, what are you doing?" shouted a concerned Mr. Frazier.

"Trying to get my little sister out of this tree if it's any of your business," he answered as he continued to jump at me.

"Lee, please stop!" I cried.

"Stop it now, boy. I'll get her down."

Lee stopped jumping at me and stood aside as Mr. Frazier lifted me to the ground. He was so tall and strong that he didn't have to stand on anything at all to help me from the tree.

"You're old man Hudson's boy, aren't you?"

"Yeah, so what?"

"You shouldn't be treating your little sister this way. You'll be sorry you did someday. Mark my words, you'll be sorry. Now you two, go on about your business. You hear?"

Lee took off running towards the store and I followed after him. I wanted my candy bar.

When I caught up with Lee, he punched me so hard he made me cry again so I stayed outside when he went in the store.

He came back out carrying a small sack filled with candy treats.

"Here; here's your old candy bar."

"I'm going to tell mommy and daddy what you did to me," I

said as I ripped the paper from the candy bar.

"You'd better not or you'll get some more," he said as he brandished his fist at me.

I did tell on him even though I knew he would continue to beat on me. He did that a lot and I didn't want to encourage his participation in his favorite hobby of punching on me, his little sister.

Mom was dressed in a bright yellowish green background calico printed dress. She grabbed a belt and gave Lee a couple of whacks for trying to push me out of the tree and getting caught by Mr. Frazier. It almost sounded like it would have been all right to push me out of the tree except that he got caught. My turn was next and I got a couple of whacks for climbing the tree.

I never climbed another tree.

Like Mr. Frazier said, Lee would be sorry he treated me badly. I've told the world what my brother was really like. I hope he is sorry about the way he treated me, but somehow I doubted it.

Nearly getting shoved out of a tree when you're a little girl plants a fear inside your head that continues to grow larger and larger as you grow up and older. I know that for a fact because it happened to me.

When I get near the edge of anything that is up high, even a staircase, it can give me the willies.

With that full blown enormous fear of heights planted firmly in my brain, how was I ever going to climb that ladder and paint the peak of our home?

Sitting at the foot of the ladder crying my eyes out wasn't going to help a bit. No, that's not quite true. It did help. It made me release a bunch of pent up tension and face facts. I was going to have to crawl up that ladder, hang on for dear life, and paint the damn thing. That's all there was to it.

I picked myself up off of the warm, inviting green grass. My legs were wobbly and my brain was numb. My hands shook as I grabbed hold of the ladder with my right hand and held the paint bucket and brush in my left hand.

Lifting my foot up to the next rung for the first two or three times was easy. After I got to the point when jumping down wouldn't be too comfortable, that's when my feet wanted to linger on each lower rung. My brain didn't want to make my feet climb any higher.

"God, help me!" I screamed as I lifted my foot to the next rung. Then I paused waiting for a bolt a lightning to come from the sky.

I took the next step a little better than the last until I realized I was past the half way point. Only a couple more feet and I could reach it, I hoped. Even if I couldn't reach it, I wasn't going up any further. I couldn't do it.

Up my shaky legs climbed and I stopped.

I didn't want to look down but I couldn't stop myself.

"Oh, God!" I cried as my knees started to buckle under me.

I grabbed onto the ladder and made myself straighten up.

I started painting. I wasn't going to stop for any reason until I was completely finished with this God-awful job.

I couldn't reach the peak, the part where the two sides of the roof came together to form a little ledge extending beyond the outside wall.

I had to climb one more step.

Quilted Memories

I screamed.

I screamed again.

One more time, I screamed.

That's what I had to do to make myself climb up another step.

I screamed the fourth time and as I was concentrating so hard on the effort it took to create the scream I stepped up one more rung.

Tears were streaming down my face as I reached up to the rafters and splashed paint on the area that had not been covered.

Done, I needed to climb no more.

That was all I had to do.

It was complete.

I had finished painting the mobile home and I continued to mumble about the rolling hillsides and mountains in southwest Virginia and why the trailer park wasn't flat.

CHAPTER 24

TOO SOON

Garfield Gold, that's the color of the block that reminds me of Aaron.

"Don't you dare, Ellen," I scolded myself. You'll only make it harder on everybody else if you start blubbering, I added as I fought back the pressure from the wave of tears I could feel building behind my eyes.

"Please don't go!" My anguished heart cried out to my youngest son, but not a sound passed through my lips begging him to stay under my roof, under my care, and under my blanket of love.

I blinked quickly, several times, fighting to control the tears. I didn't want to cry because Aaron, who is a closet softy, would also start to cry, and that was something he would try to avoid at all costs.

I watched as Aaron and Becky scurried around like mice checking this, grabbing that, and making sure they had everything including their cat "Tigger".

"You guys are late leaving. You said you wanted to be out of here by noon. It's already 1:15 PM and you're still not on the road," I said a little too harshly as I tried to cover up my pain. If I snapped and grouched at them, maybe it wouldn't hurt so much- I hoped.

I stood and stared into space remembering when Aaron had told me he had the job.

"I've got a job in Nebraska, Mom. It's what I've been looking for and what I really want," he said as he looked at his feet trying to temper his feeling of happiness.

"Nebraska!" I mouthed the word slowly making it seem as if the word had left a bad taste in my mouth. "That's so far away," I added realizing how I must have looked to my son.

"I know," he said as he kicked at something imaginary on the floor. "But I've tried and tried. I can't find anything closer. There just isn't much here in southwest Virginia that is in my computer programming field."

"I know, honey. I know. I'm just going to miss you and Becky, too," I said as I hugged him pulling my twenty-three-year-old son as close to me as I could.

Aaron and Becky, his girlfriend of several years, were large parts of my life. Watching them leave, traveling half way across the country, was almost as painful to me as it was to lose my dad when he passed on after suffering through the ravages of cancer. Unlike my father, I knew Aaron and Becky could come back, but the pain of their first parting would never leave me.

My apron strings were not the problem with Aaron leaving. It goes back much further than that.

When Aaron came into this world, he had been born via natural childbirth through no happy choice of my own. I don't like pain of any kind and would have preferred his birth having been dulled through the miracles of modern pain medication.

"Mrs. Szklarz, we can't give you anything to knock you out," explained the nurse when I asked about something to ease the pain. "You have pneumonia and we can't let you lie flat for the spinal. We can't give you anesthesia without encountering some big risks because your air passages are almost completely blocked from the swelling and congestion. You don't have any choice, Mrs. Szklarz. You'll just have to grin and bear it," she said as she walked away from the labor room bed leaving me to thrash around to my heart's content.

"I'll bear it, but I'll be loud, and I'm not going to grin," I screamed as I struggled through another long-lasting pain.

I had entered the hospital a week earlier with false labor. The emergency room doctor had let me lie for hours on an uncomfortable, lumpy cot while he made his decision about admitting me to the hospital for treatment or sending me home with a prescription clutched in my hand.

I was suffering from a bout with pneumonia that I thought was only a bad cold. I had been up day and night with Eddy, my two-year-old son, as he fought off the gut-wrenching symptoms of flu. He was so sick that I was afraid to leave him alone for any length of time. I had watched his tiny chest rise and fall as he struggled to get enough air into his lungs to stay alive.

I was afraid he would close his eyes and sleep forever.

I knew I had caught Eddy's cold, but my worry about him kept me from discovering how sick I truly was.

After I saw the arrival of Aaron, my second son, I fell into a dream-like, half-conscious state where I saw the shadows of death.

I didn't see who the person was, or if it was a person, nor did I know when the death would occur, except that it was too soon. I knew without seeing a distinguishable figure that it was one of my sons who would leave my world too soon. How much too soon, I could only guess. A feeling of an early, too soon, death filled my thoughts and shadowed my mind's eye, but that was all it was — a feeling.

I am so glad that both of my sons have endured through life to Eddy's age of thirty-seven and Aaron's age of thirty-five. I had hoped that Eddy's near death experience at the age of fifteen when the bicycle he was riding collided with a car was the answer to the premonition. It wasn't. I continued to fear the death for one of my sons, maybe even both, at an early age.

I worried about Aaron's being the reason for the warning when he was so far away that I couldn't watch over him. I never wanted to control his life or make his decisions for him, and I haven't succumbed to being the domineering mother; but I do worry about the shadows of death that I saw twenty-three years ago. I never could figure out what "too soon" was with regard to age, only that if either one of my sons dies before I do, that's too soon.

"Have you got everything?" I whispered through a voice made husky by the need to hold back the swell of tears and sobs hidden behind the lump in my throat.

"I think so; if not, you can mail it to us as soon as we

get an address," he answered loudly as he tugged at a box that was positioned precariously in the back of the rental truck.

My husband, Sonny, was helping Aaron carry, stack, and tie down everything that Aaron and Becky, his future wife and longtime girlfriend, had accumulated in their short life spans.

"Stay!" My heart cried silently as they made their preparations to move out of my life, changing my life, as I have known it for Aaron's twenty-three years.

If only he could have found a job here, then he wouldn't be traveling half way across the country to make a living, I thought sadly.

"Why couldn't he have picked a different career? What am I thinking?" I asked myself.

I molded him into the computer life by giving him an old computer to work with when he was ten. He took it apart and put it back together, making the machine sing. I was so proud of him.

I'm also proud of the fact that he taught himself the computer languages he needed along with the programming knowledge required to be hired for a job as a writer of computer programs.

It wasn't easy for him to find a job where he could use his skills. First, he had to find someone who could see beyond the fact that he was not a college graduate. He was self-taught and that was a hard to sell idea.

"Is that everything that was in the house, Becky?" shouted my blonde haired, sun-bronzed son as he reached out to grab one of the wide doors to close up the back of the truck.

"That's all I see, Aaron.   But, come and check for yourself, just to make sure."

I smiled when I heard her reply. She had learned how to handle him. Then, he has only himself to blame when something goes wrong.

I don't want anyone to misunderstand my pain caused by Aaron's leaving home. I'm not a clingy mother who dotes on her children and smothers them with too much love. The contrary is more my style.

It wasn't until Aaron's brother, Eddy, was hit by a car when he was fifteen, which was over ten years ago, that I realized I hadn't shown them very much affection at all while they were growing into manhood.

While Eddy hovered near death, I promised myself and God that I would let my boys know that I loved them. From that day forward, I always try to tell them I love them every day, even when I'm angry with them. I don't want either of my sons to ever go to bed at night with any doubt whatsoever in his mind.

If I can't tell them face to face or over the telephone wires, I tell them in my heart. But, I tell each of them "I love you" every day.

Sonny motioned and waved to Aaron as Aaron maneuvered the truck by backing it into position so he could attach the car to it using a tow-bar. With Sonny's help, they were finally ready to leave.

Aaron climbed down from the truck seat and stood in front of me as Sonny sauntered to my side.

"Mom, I love you," he said as he hugged me. "I'll miss you and dad and Eddy, too. Kiss grandma for me. Tell Eddy I'm not mad because he didn't come to see me off. Tell him I'll miss him," he said as he released me and turned his head away from me.

"I love you, too, Aaron. I'll miss you," I whispered as I forced myself not to cry.

Becky, who was holding a pet carrier containing "Tigger", lowered the carrier to the ground and hugged me with all of her might.

We had our differences, Becky and I, but I loved her because she belonged to Aaron as part of his heart. If I were to love Aaron, I had to also love Becky because she was a vital part of Aaron's life.

I willed myself not to cry.

Aaron willed himself not to cry.

Becky willed herself not to cry.

And, Sonny, my husband and Aaron's stepfather, whom Aaron just called "Dad", willed himself not to cry.

Aaron looked toward the ground, toward the truck, toward the road, toward the distant mountains, toward anything except me.

I held my chin up trying to stop the bulging tears from overflowing and rolling down my cheeks.

"Gotta go, everybody," shouted Aaron as he threw his hands into the air. "It's now or never, and, I really mean that. It is now or never."

"Never, please, never?" my heart cried.

"Be careful, Aaron. You, too, Becky. Call every time you stop for the night so we'll know you're all right. Call collect; but, please call," I shouted as they climbed into the cab of the truck

"Go with God," I whispered as I saw the bright yellow rental truck with the white car attached to the back by means of a tow-bar pulling away from my life and my watchful eyes. I knew I was asking God to watch over one of his strays. Unfortunately, Aaron has had enough education to question the reality of God, but he hasn't lived long enough to understand the need for God. That will come. I'm sure God knows that.

That big, yellow, rolling monster was swallowing up part of my life only to spit it out in Nebraska. That's so very far away from our home in the mountains of Virginia.

"I love you!" I whispered as I waved and cried while trying to smile and push my fear back into the corner, away from my real world that was falling apart before me.

"Love you, Mom, Dad," said Aaron as he put the yellow monster into gear and slowly drifted away from Sonny and me.

"I love you, too!" I shouted back knowing he couldn't hear me, but I had to say it again.

Over four years had passed and five Christmases had

been endured before I saw Aaron and Becky again. Aaron's need to support himself and the family he hopes to have someday carried him to Nebraska where he has planted the seed to grow the roots to support the blossoms of his new life. Hopefully, Aaron and Becky will be able to visit again this summer. If not, Aaron knows that I love him and always will.

Finally after all of these years, I'm having second thoughts about the shadows of death. Maybe I misread the warning. Maybe I was supposed to enjoy the young lives of my sons because the death of childhood and the birth of adulthood brought about such enormous changes for me: the loss of both of my sons to families and lives of their own.

Aaron's absence has hurt, but I know he can come home again and I still have Eddy who lives just down the road a piece.

The death of my life with my son, Aaron, came TOO SOON.

I had to fight for my sons. I'll never forget that.

My father was married twice and had created two completely different families during that time.

The first family saw the birth of Junior, Francis, Betty, and Gladys.

My brother Lee and I were issue of the second family.

The only sibling I can truly claim is Lee. The other four half-brothers and half-sisters were almost the same age as my mother. They did not want to be associated with us.

Quilted Memories

I was a divorced mother with two sons.

The father of my children had moved out of state and was far enough away not to be a problem or so I thought. He had remarried and had fathered three more sons so I hoped and prayed that he had enough family to keep himself occupied therefore leaving me and my two sons alone without any interference from him.

I stayed in contact with his mother grudgingly because she was the grandmother of my sons. When I had an emergency need for a babysitter so I could go to work, I asked Mary to watch her two grandsons until I could locate a new babysitter to replace the one who had moved away without any notice to me whatsoever.

Jude, my ex, decided he wanted to reassert his fatherhood at that time.

Without my knowledge prior to the event, Jude visited his mother and took our sons to a recreation area about fifty miles from my home where he planned, as he told his mother, to spend the day with his sons.

I called to check on the boys. That was when she told me what had happened.

"Ellen, he said he would be back late this evening. I will call you as soon as he gets here."

"Why didn't you stop him?"

"They are his sons, too."

"Yeah, I know. They are more his now than they ever were. He won't bring them back, Mary. You let him steal my babies!" I screamed into the telephone.

How she could believe him was beyond my comprehension.

"I'll call you, Ellen. Wait, you'll see. He didn't lie to me. He will be back this evening."

I waited for what seemed like a lifetime. The minutes ticked by so slowly that I called the recorded time at the local bank to check on the time. I was sure my clock had stopped along with all of my watches.

At about ten o'clock that evening my telephone finally erupted into sound. I jumped at the noisy mechanism and yelled into the receiver.

"Where are you, Jude? Where have you taken my sons?"

"I'm at my home. You're an unfit mother, Ellen. I'm keeping my sons and I'm never bringing them back to you. Say goodbye to them, now."

"Mommy, we want to come home," cried Eddy. His voice faded as if someone pulled the receiver away from his mouth.

"Mommy, come get us," screamed Aaron as he cried.

I heard the sounds of my sons no more.

"Ellen, don't be trying to get them back. I won't let you have them, never again," Jude whispered harshly. His words were dripping with hatred.

The line was dead.

Jude had taken my sons across the state line.

The telephone jangled again bringing me out of my quiet shock.

"Ellen, Jude took the boys to his house."

"I know, Mary. I want them back, now. I'm going to call the cops."

"Please don't. Ellen. I'll talk to Jude and see what he's thinking. Give me a little time to work on this. Please, Ellen, don't call the police, not yet anyway."

"He's crazy, Mary. I know he is crazy. The psychiatrist that got him excluded from the draft knew he was crazy. Why can't you believe he's crazy?"

"He's not crazy, just a little upset. Someone must have told him about something you've been doing. You know, going to the bars, sleeping with those men."

"Your crazy son has been doing all those things, Mary. That's why his live-in is pregnant."

I was crying. I couldn't talk on the telephone anymore so I hung it up as gently as I could. If I didn't, the next accusation would be that I abused her, the grandmother of my sons.

I called my mother and father.

"Mom, Jude has stolen Eddy and Aaron. He took them to his house. That's over three hundred miles from here."

"What are you going to do, Ellen?"

"I don't have any idea. If I call the police, Jude is crazy enough to hurt the boys to keep me from getting them back here. Mary said she would talk to him. I'll have to wait until morning, at least, before I make a decision," I said in between sobs.

"You're too upset to talk now. Call me back tomorrow, Ellen."

"Okay," I answered as I crumpled to the sofa succumbing to the sobs.

Mom and dad lived three hundred miles from me in the direction opposite of where Jude had taken my sons.

Later than evening, my half sister, Gladys, stopped to see dad. Mom later told me that she was very polite to her. I'll give her credit for that much kindness.

Mom told her about what had happened to my boys.

"What if I go up there and steal them back? Do you think they would come back with me?"

"I don't think so. Ellen has done a pretty good job of teaching them not to go with strangers."

"I could just snatch them up."

"You would be arrested for kidnapping, wouldn't you?"

"Yeah, I guess so, if they caught me. What else can I do to help?"

"Offering to help is more than Ellen would have ever expected. She'll get them back, one way or another."

The next day when I called mom back to tell her that Mary and Edward were going to visit Jude and would bring the boys back with them when they returned home, she told me about the offer of help that Gladys had made.

I was so surprised that they would think enough of me to even offer to do anything, let alone break the law outright.

I did get my sons back but I had to wait two whole weeks before I saw their bright shiny faces smiling at me. I stared at my babies as I watched them leap from their grandmother's car and run to my outstretched arms.

I still smile today when I think about how Gladys was going to steal my sons back for me. I shuddered to think what I would have thought had she done it, and I didn't know it was Gladys, my half-sister, that had plucked my sons from the home of their father.

If forced to do so, I wouldn't have been able to recognize her if I saw her. I hadn't seen her since I was a little girl. She was a complete stranger to me.

Gladys was the sister I wish I knew.

CHAPTER 25

TRAILER TRASH

The quilt was heavy.

It was always assumed by all that I would inherit the responsibility of taking care of my mother when my father passed from this life. Because I was the youngest and a female, the double whammy of responsibility fell directly onto my shoulders.

I didn't know that mom would change so much after dad's death. I didn't know the sweet agreeable mother and wife would turn into a demanding domineering woman who was trying to make up for all the time she lost being nice.

I also didn't know that one of the first signs of Alzheimer's was distrust for those you love most.

Mom couldn't drive a car, she didn't know how to write a check, and she didn't want to learn to do any of those things.

I acquired a sixty-one year old full grown female child when dad died at the age of seventy-four. Dad had been the man of the house therefore he made all of the financial decisions and mom liked it that way.

Quilted Memories

I kept mom with me for fourteen years and watched her grow old and ugly.

When she suffered a massive stroke I sat next to her bed and watched life leave her. The only sign of life I saw after the stroke was when she squeezed my hand the next day.

The awful arguments and the loud accusations she directed to me were what I remembered most. Those bad memories pushed away all of the good ones until I had to struggle to remember anything good that had happened between us.

The cold but weak lemonade was on the table in front of me. I watched the trails of water run down the sweating glass. I stared at the yellow liquid through water-filled eyes.

I was thinking about my brother and how much I missed him. He wasn't dead, but he might as well have been.

He was mad at me and I did not know how to undo the mad.

It all started when our mother was alive and living with me.

"Mom, get up off that bed and go take a shower," I said sternly.

"No," was the one word response. She didn't speak to me in sentences anymore because she hated me so much.

"You've got a doctor's appointment and we're not taking you to see him unless you take a shower. Do you hear me?"

"I can't."

"I'll help you. Now get up."

"I don't want you to help me."

"Fine, just take your shower."

This was a daily battle that I lost most of the time. It had been almost a month since she had taken a shower and the stench in her room and on her body was rank.

She had become incontinent and the urine smell permeated every bit of the air we breathed. Her mattress on her bed was nasty and I wanted to replace it but I wouldn't do that until I knew she would clean herself up. She wouldn't allow me to put waterproof pads beneath her to help prevent the soaking of her bedclothes and mattress. I wasn't going to waste money on a new mattress so that she could ruin it in a matter of days.

"Why am I going to the doctor?" she snapped.

"For a check-up. I need to get your prescriptions renewed," I lied.

I wanted the doctor to contact a home health service and have them send someone to the house daily to give my mother a bath, a shower, anything to help eliminate the smell that was overtaking every nook and cranny in the house.

When mom would get mad at me she would call my brother who lived almost five hundred miles away and tell him that I was abusing her.

I called home every day from work at the local school board office where I was a purchase order clerk to check on my mother and my husband who was disabled.

"Lee's here," whispered my husband.

"Why?"

"Said he just wanted to see his mother."

"Did mom call him?" I asked angrily.

"Yes."

Quilted Memories

I heaved an enormous sigh. I was fighting a losing battle.

"Do you want me to come pick you up?" asked Sonny after pausing when he heard the sigh.

"Is he staying the night?"

"No, he's leaving before you get home."

"No, don't pick me up. Let him visit mom, listen to all of her lies, and leave before I get there. He wouldn't believe anything I said anyway," I whispered as I fought the angry, hurtful, tears that were pushing against my eyes.

My brother was checking up on us, once again, because our mother had asked for help. He would make the long drive to check on her but he wouldn't take care of her. He wouldn't take her to his house to live with him for any amount of time, not even for a short visit.

It would have been a great help to us if he had taken her to visit him in his home for a week. That's all we wanted was a few days of a break from the arguments and demands.

We needed help with funeral expenses, but they weren't offered and I didn't ask. I guess he believed that we had actually stolen and used all of her money. What money he was talking about, I didn't have a clue. Her social security check paid for most of her medications.

My husband and I eventually had to file bankruptcy because I couldn't make the monthly payments to the funeral home as well as other debts and obligations that we had incurred.

My brother would not accept the fact that our mother was falling into the grasp of old age and Alzheimer's. He believed everything she said, out right, no questions asked. It wasn't fair to her and it certainly wasn't fair to me and my family who had to bear the brunt of the damage.

I wanted to explain.

I've tried to explain but the words wouldn't come. It sounded too much like a guilty person seeking forgiveness with a flimsy excuse.

I wasn't guilty. I wasn't seeking his forgiveness for treating our mother badly. I didn't want to give an excuse, only an explanation.

The letter to him was:

Dear Lee,

I loved mom and I miss you.

Ellen

I tore it up and threw it in the trash. Maybe I could write more the next time, next year on the anniversary of my mother's death.

Five years after my mother's death has not been long enough to heal the wounds caused by vicious, ugly words whispered at her funeral.

I wondered if we would be able to speak to each other after another five years had passed.

****

The tan block placed next to the dark brown block reminded me of the colors of the outside of our mobile home.

"People who live there are nothing but trash. They all are nothing but pure trash."

There was a pause as someone said something at the other end of the telephone conversation.

"I know what I'm talking about. Mobile home parks, or trailer parks, harbor people who aren't worth the powder and lead to blow them away."

There was another lull in the conversation as I stood outside the door out of the line of sight and listened.

"Up where I live they put in a trailer park next to me and those people have been nothing but trouble. They steal anything that isn't nailed down. They broke into my house when they couldn't find anything to steal outside."

Another lull occurred as I was getting so angry that I felt like exploding all over the place.

"I didn't need any proof. I know they are the ones that did it."

A pause on Mr. Reston's end of the conversation hung in the air.

"That park in Doran is the worst. Pure trash, nothing but pure trailer trash. You can't deal with those people. You just have to get rid of them. Suspend that kid each and every time you get a chance. Then maybe his family will move on to bother another school system. If we continue to do that, suspend the trouble makers in the trailer parks, maybe they'll move on out of our school system, our county, and our state."

I couldn't listen anymore. I had to walk away before I said something I would regret.

I entered my office and closed the door. I was much too angry to hold a civil conversation with any poor, unsuspecting soul who needed or wanted to talk with me.

My mind kept repeating Mr. Reston's statement about trailer park residents being trash, pure trash.

I was a mobile home park resident and specifically a resident of the trailer park in Doran.

Sure, we had some unruly people living in the area, but the same could be said about any area in the county and not just trailer park residents.

When we, my family and I, moved to Virginia from Ohio I was trying to start over in a place where my sons could grow up without the urban enticements of easy money through drug dealing and other criminal activity.

I knew where the kids my sons were hanging around with were headed. I knew my boys would be with them if I lived in Ohio very much longer.

Prison was the calling for Jason's future. Jason was Eddy's best friend. If Jason was going to follow his life's path to prison, I didn't want Eddy to share the cell.

I had family ties in southwest Virginia. There weren't many ties and they weren't very strong. Nevertheless, they were the reason I picked this area of Virginia to begin anew.

When we arrived in Virginia to stay with my Uncle Jim until we could purchase a mobile home and set it on the property that belonged to my mother through inheritance from her grandmother, we weren't welcomed with open arms.

Uncle Jim didn't want anyone around that would cause him to be accountable for his actions.

After his mother died, Uncle Jim who was my mother's brother, seemed to keep company with teenage boys and only teenage boys.

At gunpoint my uncle forced us out of the house.

The only place we could find quickly that would allow us to set up our newly purchased mobile home was the trailer park in Doran.

We left Uncle Jim's house, loading up our belongings that we had stored in the barn, and moved less the thirty miles away to Doran during a snowstorm.

We were forced into being a nomadic, transient family.

We moved into an area where we knew no one and, again, we were not welcomed with open arms.

"One of your kids keeps throwing something against my house," shouted my angry neighbor as she stood on her small porch.

"Which one?" I shouted back to her.

"I didn't see which one it was."

"Then how do you know it was my kid?"

"Just tell them to stop banging on my trailer or I'll go to the park owner."

"And what will he do?"

"He'll kick you out, you and your brats."

"How come you're so unfriendly? We've been here for over two months and this is the first time you've spoken with me."

She stepped off her porch and walked closer to me so she didn't have to shout even though she didn't leave her lot boundaries.

"My name is Ellen. My husband is Sonny. My boys are Eddy and Aaron."

"I know who you are."

"Why is everybody so unfriendly? Living here in this part of the county, the whole Richlands area, is about like living in a big city where you don't know your neighbors. Why is that?"

"You get to know somebody in a trailer park one day and then the next day they are gone. I don't waste my time on people who are just passing through."

"How long have you been here?" I asked as I glanced at her mobile home.

Her trailer was an older model but it had been well cared for and not allowed to deteriorate into a pile of neglected sheet metal.

"Ten years."

"What makes you think we won't be here that long?"

"You've got kids, and boys at that. Families with kids don't stay long. They're always moving in but they don't stay long."

"How come?"

"School problems are what I've heard."

"What kind of problems?"

"I don't know. I don't have any school age children.

She turned her back to me and walked away from me.

"I don't want your kids banging on my trailer. I'll call the landlord if they keep it up," she shouted from her small porch indicating that that was the end of the conversation.

"Eddy, Aaron," I shouted as I entered my house. They both came running into the living room.

"Have you guys been throwing or banging against that trailer next door?" I asked as I pointed toward the neighbor's house.

"I didn't mean to, mom. I didn't catch the ball," said Eddy.

"We were wrestling around earlier and my back hit the side of the trailer. I'm sorry, mom. I won't let it happen again," said Aaron.

"Don't play on that side of the house. Play on the other side or in the back, okay?"

My boys weren't angels but they didn't cause all the trouble of which they were being accused.

Mr. Reston's words cut me to the bone because I knew that we weren't trailer trash.

My kids didn't run free, deal drugs, and commit crimes.

As much as I didn't like the lady next door, her husband seemed real nice because he always spoke or waved when he saw us, I knew they weren't trailer trash.

A few bad apples got us all branded and that was so unfair.

What could I do about it?

Nothing, I couldn't do anything because it was an overheard conversation uttered by a supervisor where I worked at the school board office.

We were never accepted in that trailer park. For fifteen years we were always considered outsiders so when my mother passed away and my boys were old enough to leave home and start their own separate lives, my husband and I sold the old trailer for moving money and moved to Tazewell where we rented a house and where we were accepted by the neighbors.

Bobby lived next door and he was the nicest person you would ever want to meet.

When Sonny was hospitalized, Bobby mowed the grass for us. That's not such a big deal except that he didn't know us. He had seen the ambulance take Sonny away and when I returned home alone, he also saw that. Mowing the grass was all that he could offer to help us, his new neighbors.

"Bobby, thank you. I really appreciated your mowing the grass. Can I pay you?"

"No, that's what neighbors are for, to help each other," said the tall, slender, black man as he walked on to his mailbox to get his mail.

"Thanks, Bobby," I said again as I went back inside my house and cried. No one at the trailer park would have done that.

A few months later Sonny and I had a dream come true.

Our anniversary (eighteenth to be exact) came and went in October and no celebration was had, no gifts received, no notice was taken, no tears were shed. I gritted my teeth, said a little prayer, and proceeded to get through the day.

My fifty-third birthday passed in early November without any fanfare and, again, no material recognition. I was disappointed but finally, after all of the years of nothing, I learned to shrug it off and lived through another normal day.

Quilted Memories

It was routine for my family not to remember me on my special days. It had become my job over the years to remind everyone of upcoming birthdays and reasons for celebration with regard to anyone except me. When I chose to not remind anyone of my birthday or Mother's Day or our anniversary, I gave up my rights to remembrance. I didn't like it, but it wasn't an unusual occurrence to be passed by and forgotten.

I was usually not on the receiving end of any type of remembrance but, heaven forbid, that I should pass up any type of special day for my two grown sons and my overgrown husband. They each and every one would stand in front of me with outstretched hands when their special days arrived. They expected the recognition and celebration, especially for their birthdays, that I had lavished on each of them for years.

I'm sure it's in the genes. They weren't programmed to remember anniversaries, birthdays, and so on. They were programmed to take action only when reminded.

I wasn't going to let the thoughtless neglect by my loved ones bother me because Christmas was coming and it was going to be better than any I had ever known or ever expected to have.

I was getting a house for Christmas.

It started with the urging of my friend, Pat, for me to submit an application to the Tazewell County Habitat for Humanity over a year ago.

The process for approval was time consuming for the Habitat volunteers and the wait for a house could take years because funds must be garnered, volunteers wrangled, and the weather had to cooperate before the first nail could be driven.

During the period of waiting, my husband and I moved out of

our dilapidated mobile home where rain was leaking in on the wiring that hooked into the breaker box. We were afraid we would be burned up or burned out of our home with nothing to show for our years of toil. We moved into a rental home located over twenty miles closer to my place of employment. Distance from work was no problem for my husband because he was disabled. We continued to wait not having much hope that we would really be considered for a house.

The Habitat House that had been built in Tazewell three years earlier was occupied by a young mother who married and wanted to start her new life with her new husband in a new and different home. She left the Habitat House to be recycled and resold to waiting applicants.

Thank you to all of you who allowed our name and number to pop up giving us an opportunity to thrust our roots into the ground. We no longer were members of the transient society in Tazewell County who lived in mobile homes and rental dwellings.

We could gladly start the process of fixing up, painting, and getting ready to move to our Christmas present that would be like no other that we might ever receive in our lifetimes.

We were in our home by Christmas and no other thoughts, wishes, or presents were necessary.

Stop in to see us if you want to see a happy couple oozing with good will and best wishes. We don't have a lot, but we'll share with you what we can.

It sure was nice to feel accepted and to know that we were no longer considered trailer trash. Let me reassure you, I never was trailer trash!

Now – the only one left in my Habitat house is me. I'm doing my best to try to change the house from our home to my home.

It's a long, hard process, but I have to do it to eradicate the ghosts of Sonny rambling around the house and making me sad.

CHAPTER 26

I AM MOM

A startling realization slammed into me forcing me to write another letter that would never be mailed. This memory was totally due to tan and brown squares scattered throughout my quilt.

Oh, by the way, mom, do you remember me as a little girl who loved you with all of her heart? I think I do.

Now, I'm trying to figure out what happened to change everything.

I remember asking you why you didn't drive?

You told me it wasn't necessary because dad did all the driving.

Do you remember telling me "You have to ask your dad" every time I asked to go anywhere or do anything?

Do you remember me asking why we never went anywhere or had any friends?

Going to stay all night with relatives wasn't going anywhere fun. We never, ever went to an amusement park or to a zoo or a movie with you and dad. Why was that, mom?

If I wanted to have a friend to come to the house to play, you told me "NO". Why did that always happen?

If I wanted to play my records, why was I never allowed to do so until you both weren't in the house?

Why did you blame dad for every disappointment?

Now - I know why my feelings toward you changed.

I grew up.

I swore with all of my heart that I would never, ever be like you.

I married and gave birth to two beautiful sons who loved me with every ounce of strength that they had in their tiny bodies.

I did learn to drive but I hate to do so.

My boys weren't directed to ask their father every time they had to go anywhere or do anything. They didn't have a father around the house all the time that could take the blame for any disappointments because we were divorced.

Because I hated to go stay with relatives, my boys and I didn't get to do very much because I couldn't afford the cost of the pleasures of amusement parks or zoos or movies.

I didn't have time for the friends of my sons. I didn't have time to make a bunch of little boys happy because I worked all of the time.

I wasn't a stay at home mom like you. I had to work and make a living to support myself and my two sons even while I was married. I dreamed of having that opportunity of staying at home and watching each of my sons take his first step and say his first word.

I could play my music anytime I felt like it which wasn't very often because I tended to listen to the words of the music and be reminded of sadder times. The sad memories brought on by the music pushed me further into a depression that I struggled to stay out of at all times.

I didn't have a husband to blame for all the disappointments and mistakes I made with my sons.

And, oh, by the way, mom, I think I finally understand.

I am mom.

Will you forgive me?

Love always,

Ellen

CHAPTER 27

JUST AS I AM

Next came the depression the dark feelings represented by the dark squares in the quilt.

Does anybody out there really, I mean R-E-A-L-L-Y like me? I'm talking about the stern, demanding, and larger than life person that I am or appear to be to my family members and coworkers.

"She's such a b---h," is a phrase I have heard more than once in my lifetime.

"Don't tell mom, she'll get mad," is another phrase that I have grown to hate.

Not all of us can have a sparkling, bubbly, and syrupy sweet personality. The constantly smiling, giggling female can't be real - can she? I mean, no one can expect life to be the proverbial bowl of cherries all the time. As a matter of fact, my thoughts seem to place emphasis on the "Pits".

Even though you characterize me as a "Grouch" or "Loner", I have feelings just like anyone else. You may not be aware that I am capable of feeling anything other than disappointment and regret, but I feel every harsh word that takes wing and plunges into my heart adding another pain that will never go away.

I am a serious minded individual who has tried to change and become what others would have me to be. My exterior demeanor is my defense mechanism and once this shield is removed, I become so very vulnerable to all kinds of emotional pain.

I am a proud woman. I don't want you to see any signs of weakness in me. It's my job to take care of my family and it's my job to perform my duties to the best of my abilities at my place of employment.

Please remember that people like me can be hurt. We can cry even though you probably will never see it. We don't always want to be the loner you think we are, but it's a lot easier to avoid the pain of rejection than be made aware of it in every way.

I don't want to be stern and demanding, but you, who see me that way, force me to live that role.

On several occasions my coworkers have forgotten about me when a celebratory luncheon was planned.

On one specific occasion, I didn't know everyone had already left for the restaurant until I walked to the lobby.

"Has everybody left?" I asked Penny, the professional, older lady sitting at the reception desk.

She was a supervisor who was kind enough to fill in for the receptionist who had gone to the luncheon.

"Oh, yes, about fifteen minutes ago," she responded. "I

thought you were going to go?" she asked with a lilt.

"I did, too," I whispered as I walked away fighting back the tears of being the forgotten one.

Penny followed me to my office.

"Do you want to go with me?" she asked, knowing that I didn't have my car, and she was feeling sorry for me. "I'm going to meet them when Sam gets here to take over phone duties."

"No, thank you. I don't like to go anywhere late, and I especially don't like going where I'm obviously not welcome," I answered struggling to maintain control and not cry - not in front of Penny. I prefer to cry in private.

"You're welcome to come with me," she shouted as she walked rapidly to the receptionist's desk to answer the insistent phone that was jingling my nerves.

I am a real person who needs to be loved and to love. I'm not the bubbly fountain of happiness you think I should be. I've tried all my life to change, but it's not going to happen - can't you accept me just as I am?

I only demand from my coworkers and family what I expect of myself. I know that if I can do a certain task, that they can do the same task. I wouldn't ask anyone to do what I couldn't or wouldn't do myself. Of course, I can't jump out of airplanes or climb Mount Everest, and I would not expect you to do either of those feats. I can write a decent letter and I can add a column of figures accurately. I'm sure you can do the same.

I can love and accept my family members as they are and I know they can do the same for me and not be afraid of me - why are they afraid? I don't bite. I don't yell very often, either; but I do love them very, very much and I try to tell them that, especially my sons and husband, daily.

I don't know why my sons are afraid of my reactions when they have to tell me something they think I might not be happy about.

I don't spring into a reaction by slapping, hitting, paddling, cursing, or being generally ugly. I took after my father in that way. It just took a look, a certain look, and my brother and I were walking the straight and narrow path to his good graces.

I sit and listen to what my son has to say. If I don't like what he has told me, I tell him so and that we will have to discuss it later. I need time to think and sort out his words and reasoning behind what he has done.

I also discovered early on in my parenting years that my sons learned more about what they did that was wrong if they had time to stew about what my reaction would be. What form of punishment would I mete out to them in retribution for their bad deed?

In many cases, I had to do nothing else to punish them. Stewing was enough.

Stewing also made them aware of what might happen and I believe that's what they are afraid of - not what does happen.

With my coworkers I appear to be a loner, but I'm not that way at all. I can't afford to go out to lunch every day. Twice a month is about all I wish to waste on costly lunches outside of the office. I have too many responsibilities away from the office to throw my hard-earned money away on that kind of extravagant momentary pleasure.

On a nice day in September not too long ago, a question was thrown out in the lobby to anyone of us women who happened by about when we should have our next gathering to draw secret pal names from a hat. The drawing would last the full year with no one telling whose name they had until the gathering for the drawing to be held the next year. At the gathering, the secret pals would be revealed and new names chosen. You would then buy cards and gifts for whatever holidays occurred as well as for birthdays and anniversaries.

The first year we began our secret pal activity in the third week of November. When the new date was being scheduled, I mentioned that it should be at about the same time for the new drawing because there were a couple of people who had birthdays between November 3rd, the new date, and the date chosen the previous year, November 21st.

You had to know that I was one of those forgotten birthdays. The other person whose birthday fell into that time frame was not participating.

I was very hurt when I was left out of the first year, but I continued to participate in the activity. I always made sure I didn't leave my secret pal out of any celebration. I'll not participate next year with no trace of sour grapes leaving a bad taste with anyone except me.

I have a lot of work to do and lengthy lunch hours drag me down, make me sluggish, and I don't want to come back to the office back to the daily grind. Working is what I get paid for - not chitchat with my coworkers. I don't mean that in a negative way. It's only the truth.

I have a very strong work ethic that was ingrained into me by my father and my first employer. I can't forget what I was taught about being on time and doing the tasks for which I am being paid, nor do I want to forget them.

I don't have time for all of the fun and games while I'm working. Maybe it would be nice if I did have the time, but I would only feel guilty.

I hurt when harsh, cruel words are hurled at me but my shield is the impenetrable front I display around those who can get to me the most.

I'm not the mean, ugly, ogre you want to believe that I am - I am me - a real, live, breathing person who has a heart that can be hurt. Accept me just as I am – that's how I accept you.

I did participate in the Secret Santa drawing again, and again, and again.

****

"Can you imagine having a large family?" I asked myself as I wandered through the discount store aisles watching people load shopping buggies with mountains of gifts. "No, never had one, never," I responded to my own question.

Sonny and I were going to be alone again for the holidays.

The small town in which we lived was filled with large families, small families, and blended families. Not many inhabitants of the town were alone, except for each other, like Sonny and I.

"Let's do Secret Santa this year," said the boss lady, Barbara, as she tried to force the Christmas spirit onto those under her supervision.

"That's a great idea," gushed several of the ladies to whom the Secret Santa remark was aimed. What else could they say? It was, after all, the boss lady's suggestion.

"The Secret Santa events in which I participated in the past consisted of a week of gift giving. There would be four consecutive days of small, inexpensive gifts given by each Secret Santa followed by a significant gift on the fifth day of say between

273

ten and fifteen dollars. We will all gather together in my office on the fifth day and reveal to each other the Secret Santa's. Nancy will list each name on small pieces of paper for each of us to choose for whom we are to be Secret Santa. If you don't wish to participate, let Nancy know so your name will not be added to the pot."

I wasn't keen on the idea but what the heck, I'll give it another try. At least I could be a part of a little almost family activity. My coworkers were my family, with the exception of Sonny who had become my life.

I wrapped the small snowman shaped candy dish and slipped it into Diana's interoffice mailbox on the first day of gift giving.

I checked my mailbox and found a small unwrapped box of paper liners for muffin baking cups. I looked at the gift and quickly stuffed it into my pocket so no one would see what I had received. It embarrassed me to believe that someone I worked with could be so thoughtless.

"Pam, is that what you got from your Secret Santa?" I asked the lady in the neighboring office who was displaying a holiday figurine on her desk.

"Yes, it is. Isn't it really nice? I've got a good Secret Santa. What did you get?"

"I'll show you later. It's in my office."

The second day of gift giving, I gave Diana a large solid chocolate Santa.

I received an unwrapped box of small zipper storage bags.

"What did you get today, Ellen?"

"Storage bags."

When anyone asked me about the gifts I received, I told them how I felt. "My Secret Santa is sick."

Day three arrived and I gave Diana a snowman coffee mug filled with individually wrapped small candies.

I received muffin flour mix.

The fourth day, I gave Diana a dark blue Christmas kitchen towel wrapped in bright paper.

I received a pair of elf socks adorned with bells that I wore around the office to appease whoever might be my Secret Santa.

Day five, the gathering was to happen and I did not want to know who might be my Secret Santa.

When I arrived at my office, I found two envelopes on my desk.

Ellen, Envelope #1:

The envelope attached represents the caring and spirit of the season that I would like to share with you. Please accept this from me as my gift to you with no hard feelings about comments made. Sharing of the heart is one of the best gifts one person can give another and today I have shared my heart with you.

Happy holidays from someone who cares.

Ellen, Envelope #2:

$20.00 gift certificate to local steak house

At the gathering I held my last gift for Diana on my lap until it became Diana's turn to identify herself to the person for whom she had been Secret Santa. Diana was very pleased with the snowman music box she received from me.

Karen, my Secret Santa, handed me a delicate Christmas tree ornament. I thanked Karen for all the gifts which included muffin papers, food storage bags, flour, and the socks. I made no mention of the gift certificate. I couldn't do that without crying.

I carried those two envelopes around with me for months to remind myself that I should never voice my personal opinion in public again.

"Next year will be better," I thought finally without the tears.

CHAPTER 28

THE NIGHTSTAND

The dark green blocks of the quilt became the center of attention.

The paint wasn't even dry on the nightstand that I always kept beside my bed when I hauled it back into the house for fear that someone would come along and take my precious possession. I had painted it a dark hunter green with paint I had purchased from the local dollar store.

It looked so much better with the coat of green paint that covered the water stains and scratches that came along with years and years of use and abuse. Unlike the choice of the uppity decorators of the moneyed set who preferred the distressed look, I always went along with my dad's theory that if it started to look old and neglected, throw a little paint on it to spruce it up a bit. Usually buying a new replacement was not an option, so I was taught to take care of what I had.

"What are you going to do with that?" asked my husband.

Quilted Memories

"Put it back where it came from, right beside my bed."

"Don't you think it should go into the trash? If not the trash, put it in the storage building or use it on the back porch for a plant table."

"I can't do that. It is a connection to my dad. This thing is years and years old. Dad found it along side of the road where someone else had thrown it out. He needed a night stand so he took it home for his own use.

"See that hole there? On the edge? This is actually the left side of a larger dresser. It was a piece of the cutwork that had been part of the original dresser. I bet you didn't know that."

"No, I never thought about it before until you pointed it out. I always thought it was a mistake in cutting the wood somewhere along the way through the building process."

"This little nightstand with its three drawers held all of dad's personal and important possessions. In it he would place his wallet, his pocket knife, his loose change, and anything else he felt the need to squirrel away into his pant pockets," I said as my eyes glistened momentarily with the pain of missing him.

"I didn't know your dad very well. He died soon after we were married."

"You would have liked him if you had gotten to know him. He didn't have much to say to anybody until it was important. He did not interfere in my life in any way except to love me."

"It's still ugly. It really should go. You know that," he said softly without trying to incur my wrath.

"After dad died, mom took over possession of the nightstand. She is the one who water spotted it and scratched it up. Mom never was too careful with anything and that included furniture."

"Yeah, she didn't care too much about anything towards the end except eating. Old age had affected her mind really bad. She acted okay with me, but she truly hated you, her own daughter. You - we were the only persons in the world trying to keep her healthy and alive and she truly resented it. She was ready to die long before we allowed her to die. She gave up a year earlier while we were still, especially you, trying to get her to move around and keep her muscles active and working."

"I know she didn't know what she was doing or saying at the end, but it hurt to see the mean, hateful looks she would throw at me and hear the "I hate you" words whispered to me daily," the good glistening tears for my dad were replaced with hard, angry tears as I fought to control the tone of my voice.

"I would think the bad memories of your mother would be reason enough to trash the nightstand."

"Yes, it would be if I allowed that to happen. Even though the bad memories are all consuming sometimes, I remember when my best friend envied me because of my mom. Sandy Gore told me that she wished her mom was just like mine. I remember the smiles and the attempts at making me and my brother happy.

"We didn't have much money, but mom did her best. So did dad, but because of progress and the rapid influx of machines replacing the jobs of the able-bodied men, dad was laid off from his job time and time again. It was a struggle for him to remain employed."

"Okay, okay, keep the thing. But the least you could do is find someone to replace the top and get rid of the deep crack in the wood in the center of the top. You can't place a glass of water on that table anywhere near that crack without fear of it tipping over with the slightest bump against that table. All of the years of paint could be removed and it could be refinished properly, making it look good."

"It's got a fresh coat of paint. I want the crack to stay with it. Mom is the reason for the crack. She kept spilling water on the table and it finally dried up one day and cracked open like it was trying to tell her to be more careful. It didn't work though. She was still sloppy and careless."

"Okay, okay, say you keep it until the day you die. You're fifty seven years old now and your boys are in their thirty's. What will happen to it then, after you die, I mean?"

"Eddy or Aaron will take it. Most likely it will be Eddy because he is a little more sentimental than Aaron."

"You're kidding, aren't you?"

"Nope, if I leave nothing else to my sons and that looks like what will happen at the rate we're going living from paycheck to paycheck; at least one of them will have the hunter green nightstand and the memories of a grandfather, a grandmother, and a mother to encourage him to keep it with him. Not much of a material legacy, I know, but the stories of the lives that have survived around this nightstand could fill pages of books.

"I want this nightstand to be a reminder of who went before him and why he is here now."

I carried the nightstand to the bedroom where I slowly refilled it with trinkets and memories from the past.

The bottom drawer contained my dad's pocket knives and pocket watches that were almost appendages to his body. He had one on his person every day of his life. His last driver's license was lying beside dad's items to let my sons know who the items belonged to when the sorting of my life's accumulations began in earnest.

The second drawer held trinkets from my mother's life. There was a baby shoe from my brother and me, a silver ring with a couple of blue stones she gave to me a couple of months before her death, and her old set of wedding rings. She went to meet her Maker with the newest set dad had bought her.

The third drawer is mine. It holds baubles, bangles, and ribbons from various points of my life that I will keep near me until the importance rubs off and is replaced by a newer and better memory. Some items such as the pictures of each of my newborn sons will never be removed while other pieces of memories will fade and be moved from my drawer. Another item that will continue to stay in that drawer is the direction to the location of <u>The Little Old Lady Next Door</u>. It is an autobiography that covers my first forty years. The second volume, <u>Watch Out for Eddy</u>, is the story of my sons. A third volume, the one you are now reading, explains why I have become who I am today. If and when either or both of them want to read about how they came into being, the information is there for them - my legacy to my sons.

The nightstand will remain part of the history of my family as long as I am alive. I hope one of my sons sees fit to keep it as a remembrance long after I'm gone.

When I crawled into bed that night, I could smell the fresh paint that had been applied to the nightstand, just like my dad would have done, and I smiled.

CHAPTER 29

VISIONS

I looked out the window, daydreaming about what might have been. It didn't matter anymore about what I wanted to do; only what I could do was important.

My eyes filled with a mist that blurred my sight into the world outside that pane of glass, but I could see clearly the visions that danced through my ever active brain, taunting and enticing me to sit down and bring those scenarios to life.

Occasionally I would pick up a piece of paper and begin to write what I could see as clearly as if I were sitting in the local movie theater, except these stories were fresh and new and the people were real.

I was like a mystic, a teller of future truths, but I gave the truths life by setting them to paper like a musician causes the birth of a new song by scribing the notes to lined sheets for safe keeping.

I had always wanted to be a writer. That was my dream, my daydream. Was I getting too old for the dream to matter? I had always made excuses about why I didn't write.

Excuse number one:

"I don't have time with trying to take care of a husband and two sons."

Excuse number two:

"Nobody will want to read what I've got to say."

Excuse number three:

"I'm a nobody, a dreamer. I have to face reality and put this silliness out of my head."

There were also excuses number four through forever.

I am a clerk in my sixties, long past the dreams of my youth.

Now, my excuses were fewer. I had time to write and put my thoughts and ideas to paper to leave as a legacy for my two sons.

Now, I would face the rejection from people who were smarter than I was, better educated, and much more respected for having succeeded with their choices of livelihood. Could I withstand the rejection and dejection? I would never know unless I tried.

My visions were never about my own life – well - maybe a little. There were always stories to tell about those around me and how things might have turned out under a different set of circumstances.

One of my favorites was the story of my Uncle Jim. He was a mean man of questionable character. He seemed to favor the company of teenage boys. Nothing was ever said about whether my suspicions were true or not but deep down in my heart I knew they were. I managed to write a novel and entitled it An Awfully Lonely Place that was published by PublishAmerica.

Quilted Memories

I had written the book about my Uncle Jim and had murdered him off as a way of eliminating someone in my life that I didn't like. I had also burned the old home place down to the ground as part of the cover-up. Of course, my Uncle Jim was still alive and kicking at the ripe old age of seventy-five when I finished writing my book because I never meant for anything bad to happen to him.

Unfortunately, the old house did burn to the ground leaving the chimney standing as a marker of the passing of a legacy that would go no further. When I saw the charred remains and the lone chimney reaching upward for help from the sky, I realized I had described my vision of the scene years earlier in my book.

After much soul searching, I knew I could succeed. Now was the time to try and keep trying, mailing and remailing my manuscripts until someone could see in them what I knew I had buried deep in my soul.

The postmaster must have loved to see me arrive at the window each time I could find an address to send my manuscript. Occasionally I could see pity in the eyes of those who were taking my precious hard earned money to pay for the postage to mail a two hundred fifty to six hundred page manuscript. Most of my manuscripts were short stories but when I felt I could afford it, I would take a chance on the larger more costly mailings.

Several of my short stories were published for little or no payment. That didn't matter because I was trying to get my name out into the mainstream. I was trying to become recognized on the Internet. I wanted a future publishing possibility to be able to type in my name into the computer and pull up a listing of awards given to me by others who thought me worthy of recognition.

I, the purchase order clerk have not missed my calling. I, the purchase order clerk, am a published novelist.

Now, I will be known as an author, a writer of words that mean something, and not just a purchase order clerk for the Tazewell County School System.

Now, I have a real legacy for my two sons.

CHAPTER 30

THE BEGINNING OF THE END

In order to quell all of the bad memories, I knew I had to get rid of the quilt. Yes, there were some good memories, but the bad far outweighed the good.

I removed the quilt from my bed and stored it in a secure box for safekeeping.

One day I will give that quilt to one of my sons as a remembrance of his grandmother.

I know my son will have only good memories of his grandmother and the quilt will not be able to manipulate and control his dreams.

ABOUT THE AUTHOR

 Linda Hoagland has won acclaim for her mystery novels that include *Snooping Can Be Doggone Deadly* and *Crooked Road Stalker.* She is also the author of works of nonfiction, a collection of short writings, along with a volume of poems. Hoagland has won numerous awards for her work including first place for the Pearl S. Buck Award for Social Change and the Sherwood Anderson Short Story Contest twice. She is currently the president of the Appalachian Authors Guild.

You can purchase Linda's work on her website:

lindasbooksandangels.com

SEE THE LIST OF LINDA'S BOOKS ON THE FOLLOWING PAGES.

FICTION

ONWARD AND UPWARD

SNOOPING CAN BE DOGGONE DEADLY

SNOOPING CAN BE DEVIOUS

SNOOPING CAN BE CONTAGIOUS

SNOOPING CAN BE DANGEROUS

THE BEST DARN SECRET

CROOKED ROAD STALKER

CHECKING ON THE HOUSE

DEATH BY COMPUTER

THE BACKWARDS HOUSE

AN AWFULLY LONELY PLACE

Linda Hudson Hoagland

NONFICTION

MISSING SAMMY

90 YEARS AND STILL GOING STRONG

QUILTED MEMORIES

LIVING LIFE FOR OTHERS

JUST A COUNTY BOY: DON DUNFORD

WATCH OUT FOR EDDY

THE LITTLE OLD LADY NEXT DOOR

COLLECTIONS

I AM...LINDA ELLEN

A COLLECTION OF WINNERS

Quilted Memories